Dropshipping Unboxed:

Revealing The Secrets To Success

By Alexander J. Kelley

Dropshipping Unboxed: Revealing the Secrets to Success

Copyright © 2023 by Alexander J. Kelley

Book Cover by Alexander J. Kelley

First Edition 2003

www.alexanderkelley.com

To my wife, Laura.
Every day with you is a gift. Thank you for being my rock.
I love you.

Table of Contents

Chapter 1: Introduction to Dropshipping

Chapter 1

What Dropshipping Is & Why It's a Popular Business Model

Dropshipping is a popular business model that has gained significant traction in recent years. It is a retail fulfillment method where a store doesn't keep the products it sells in stock. Instead, when a store sells a product, it purchases the item from a third party and has it shipped directly to the customer. This means that the store doesn't have to worry about inventory management or shipping logistics.

The appeal lies in its simplicity and low cost of entry. Unlike traditional retail models, dropshipping doesn't require a lot of upfront capital. Store owners don't have to invest in inventory, which can be a significant cost barrier for many entrepreneurs. This means that anyone can start a business from anywhere in the world with just an internet connection.

Another reason why it is popular is that it allows store owners to offer a wide range of products without having to deal with the hassle of stocking and managing inventory. With dropshipping, you can easily add new products to your store without worrying about the costs of buying and storing the products.

It also offers a lot of flexibility. Since you don't have to handle inventory, you can run your business from anywhere, whether it's your home, a coffee shop, or a co-working space. This means that you can work from anywhere in the world and set your own schedule.

However, dropshipping is not without its challenges. One of the biggest challenges is the risk of stockouts and supplier issues. Since you are relying on a third-party supplier to fulfill your orders, you have little control over the quality of the products and the shipping times. This can lead to unhappy customers and a negative reputation for your store.

Additionally, since the cost of entry is low, dropshipping has become a highly competitive market. This means that you need to have a solid marketing and sales strategy to stand out from the competition and attract customers.

Overall, dropshipping is a popular business model because it offers a low-cost, low-risk way to start an e-commerce business. With the right strategy and execution, it can be a profitable and scalable business model that offers a lot of flexibility and freedom for entrepreneurs. In the following chapters, we will explore how to get started and how to build a successful business.

Chapter 1

Brief History of Dropshipping

While dropshipping has become popular in recent years, the concept has been around for much longer than many people realize. In fact, dropshipping can be traced back to the mail-order catalogs of the late 19th century.

Back then, companies like Sears and Montgomery Ward would print catalogs and allow customers to order products directly from the catalog. These companies would then fulfill the orders by shipping products directly from the manufacturer to the customer.

The modern concept of dropshipping as we know it today, however, started to take shape in the early 2000s. At the time, e-commerce was still in its infancy, and many entrepreneurs were looking for ways to start an online business without having to invest a lot of money upfront.

One of the first companies to popularize the dropshipping model was Amazon. In 2006, Amazon launched its FBA (Fulfillment by Amazon) program, which allowed sellers to store their products in Amazon's warehouses and have Amazon handle the fulfillment and shipping of their orders. While not a traditional dropshipping model, FBA paved the way for the rise of third-party fulfillment services and made it easier for sellers to start an e-commerce business without having to worry about inventory management and shipping logistics.

Around the same time, AliExpress, a subsidiary of Alibaba, was also gaining traction. AliExpress allowed Chinese manufacturers to sell directly to consumers all around the world. This opened a whole new world of products for dropshippers and made it possible for entrepreneurs to start a business with very little upfront investment.

The rise of platforms like Shopify and WooCommerce also played a significant role in the industry's growth. These platforms made it easy for anyone to set up an online store without having to worry about the technical aspects of building and managing a website.

Today, dropshipping has become a popular business model for entrepreneurs all around the world. It offers a low-cost, low-risk way to start an online business, and it's a great way to test the waters before committing to a larger inventory-based business.

Chapter 1

Advantages and Disadvantages

Like any business model, dropshipping has its advantages and disadvantages. Let us explore both sides of the coin.

Advantages:

1. Low Startup Costs: One of the biggest advantages is the low startup costs. You don't need to invest in inventory upfront, which means you can start your business with very little capital.
2. No Inventory Management: No need to worry about storing and managing inventory. This means you don't need to invest in warehouse space or worry about inventory management software.
3. Wide Product Selection: With dropshipping, you can sell a wide variety of products without needing to invest in the inventory upfront. This means you can offer your customers a broad selection of products and test different products without committing to a large inventory.
4. Location Independence: Operate your business from anywhere in the world, as long as you have an internet connection. This means you can work from home, travel, or work from a co-working space.
5. Flexibility: With dropshipping, you have the flexibility to test different products, suppliers, and marketing strategies without a lot of upfront costs or commitments.

Disadvantages:

1. Lower Profit Margins: One of the biggest disadvantages is the lower profit margins. Since you're not buying products in bulk, you're not getting the same discounts as wholesalers or retailers, which means your profit margins will be lower.
2. Lack of Control: With dropshipping, you don't have control over the quality of the products or the shipping process. This means that if a supplier messes up an order, it's your business that will suffer.
3. Supplier Dependence: One drawback is that you're dependent on your suppliers to fulfill orders and ship products. This means that if

a supplier goes out of business, you'll need to find a new supplier quickly.

4. Shipping Costs: With dropshipping, you'll need to pay for shipping costs, which can eat into your profit margins.

5. Customer Service: Even though the customer is receiving the product directly from someone else, you're ultimately responsible for customer service, which means you'll need to handle any issues that arise with your customers.

Dropshipping offers many advantages for entrepreneurs looking to start an online business with little upfront investment. However, it also has its disadvantages, and it's important to weigh both sides of the coin before deciding if this is the right business model for you. In the next chapter, we will explore the different types and how they work.

Chapter 2: Getting Started with Dropshipping

Chapter 2

Different Types of Dropshipping and How They Work

There are several different types of dropshipping, each with its own unique advantages and disadvantages. In this chapter, we'll explore the different types and how they work.

1. AliExpress Dropshipping: AliExpress is a popular marketplace that connects buyers with suppliers in China. With AliExpress dropshipping, you can list products for sale on your website or e-commerce platform and then order those products from suppliers on AliExpress. The supplier will then ship the product directly to your customer.

2. Oberlo Dropshipping: Oberlo is a popular app that allows you to import products from AliExpress and other marketplaces directly into your e-commerce store. With Oberlo dropshipping, you can easily add products to your store and fulfill orders with just a few clicks.

3. Amazon Dropshipping: Amazon dropshipping involves listing products for sale on Amazon and then ordering those products from a supplier when a customer places an order. The supplier will then ship the product directly to your customer.

4. Private Label Dropshipping: Private label dropshipping involves working with a manufacturer to create a custom product that you can sell under your own brand name. The manufacturer will handle the production and shipping of the product.

5. Print on Demand Dropshipping: Print on demand dropshipping involves creating custom products like t-shirts, mugs, or phone cases, and then having a supplier print and ship those products when a customer places an order.

6. Wholesale Dropshipping: Wholesale dropshipping involves buying products from a wholesaler at a discounted price and then selling those products at a markup. The wholesaler will handle the shipping of the product directly to your customer.

Each type has its own unique advantages and disadvantages. Some are better suited for certain types of products, while others may be more profitable depending on the market and competition. It's important to do your research and choose the right type for your business.

Chapter 2

Choosing A Dropshipping Platform or Marketplace

Choosing the right dropshipping platform or marketplace is crucial to the success of your business. In this chapter, we'll explore how to choose the right platform for your needs.

1. Consider Your Needs: The first step in choosing a dropshipping platform or marketplace is to consider your needs. Do you want a platform that offers a wide selection of products or one that's focused on a specific niche? Do you need a platform that offers automated order fulfillment or one that requires more manual work? Consider factors like pricing, ease of use, and customer support.

2. Research Platforms: Once you've identified your needs, it's important to research platforms that meet those needs. Look for platforms that have a good reputation and that have been in business for a while. Read reviews and ask for recommendations from other dropshippers.

3. Evaluate Pricing: Pricing is an important factor to consider when choosing a dropshipping platform or marketplace. Look for platforms that have transparent pricing and that don't charge hidden fees. Consider factors like transaction fees, monthly fees, and shipping costs.

4. Look for Integrations: If you're using other tools like an ecommerce platform or a payment gateway, it's important to look for dropshipping platforms that integrate with those tools. This can help you streamline your business and avoid double data entry.

5. Consider Customer Support: Customer support is an important factor to consider when choosing a dropshipping platform or marketplace. Look for platforms that offer responsive customer support and that have a good track record of resolving issues quickly.

6. Try Before You Buy: Many dropshipping platforms and marketplaces offer free trials or demos. Take advantage of these offers to test out the platform and see if it meets your needs.

Overall, the top dropshipping companies tend to have a strong focus on customer satisfaction, efficient order processing, and quality products, all of which are essential for building a successful and sustainable business. Most offer a wide range of products from different categories to cater to a broader customer base, while offering high-quality products from reputable suppliers, which helps to ensure customer satisfaction and repeat business. Here is a list of the Top 20 dropshipping platforms or marketplaces as of 2023:

1. Oberlo - Oberlo is unique in that it is a Shopify app that offers a seamless integration with the platform. This makes it easy for merchants to start dropshipping on Shopify without the need for a separate platform or software. Oberlo also offers a user-friendly interface that simplifies the process of finding and importing products from AliExpress. Additionally, it provides various features such as order tracking, pricing automation, and product customization options to help merchants optimize their dropshipping business.

2. Spocket - Spocket sets itself apart from other dropshipping companies by focusing on providing merchants with high-quality, US/EU-based suppliers. This means that merchants can offer their customers faster shipping times, higher quality products, and a more reliable service overall. Spocket also offers a user-friendly interface that simplifies the process of finding and importing products from suppliers. Additionally, it provides various features such as real-time inventory updates, order tracking, and branded invoicing to help merchants streamline their dropshipping business.

3. SaleHoo - SaleHoo sets itself apart from other dropshipping companies by offering a directory of verified suppliers that have been thoroughly vetted by its team. This means that merchants can have peace of mind knowing that they are working with reliable and trustworthy suppliers. SaleHoo's directory includes a wide range of products, including electronics, fashion, and home goods. Additionally, it provides various tools and resources to help merchants start and grow their dropshipping business, such as

market research tools, product sourcing guides, and community forums.

4. Doba - Doba is a dropshipping platform that provides merchants with access to over two million products from a variety of suppliers. Doba's unique feature is its product sourcing tool, which allows merchants to search for and find products that are in high demand and have a low level of competition. Additionally, it provides various features such as order management, inventory updates, and real-time product data to help merchants streamline their dropshipping business.

5. Wholesale2B - Wholesale2B is a dropshipping platform that offers a variety of products, including electronics, fashion, and home goods. One of its unique features is its integration with over 100 dropshipping suppliers, which gives merchants access to a wide range of over 1.5 million products and suppliers to choose from. Additionally, it provides various features such as real-time inventory updates, order tracking, and automatic product data updates to help merchants manage their dropshipping business more efficiently. It is user-friendly, and it offers a 7-day free trial.

6. AliExpress - AliExpress is a popular online marketplace that offers a wide range of products from suppliers based in China and other parts of the world. It provides various features and tools to help merchants find and import products, including a product sourcing tool, product recommendations, and automated order fulfillment. Additionally, AliExpress offers competitive pricing and a vast selection of products, including electronics, fashion, and home goods.

7. Modalyst - Modalyst is a dropshipping platform that offers a range of products, including fashion, beauty, and home goods. One of its unique features is its integration with a network of suppliers that offer unique and niche products, such as sustainable fashion and artisanal home goods. Additionally, Modalyst provides various features such as real-time inventory updates, automatic order fulfillment, and customized branding options to help merchants manage their dropshipping business more efficiently.

8. Printful - Printful is a dropshipping platform that specializes in on-demand printing and embroidery services for apparel, home decor, and accessories. One of its unique features is its ability to seamlessly integrate with eCommerce platforms such as Shopify and WooCommerce, allowing merchants to create custom products and designs that can be printed and shipped directly to their customers. Additionally, Printful provides various features such as real-time shipping rates, order tracking, and product mockups to help merchants manage their dropshipping business more efficiently.

9. CJDropshipping - CJDropshipping (cont.) - CJDropshipping is a dropshipping platform that offers a range of products, including electronics, fashion, and beauty products. One of its unique features is its integration with various eCommerce platforms, including Shopify, WooCommerce, and eBay. This allows merchants to easily manage their inventory, track their orders, and automate their shipping processes. Additionally, CJDropshipping offers a range of tools and resources to help merchants find and import products from its network of suppliers, including a product sourcing tool and a custom branding service.

10. Worldwide Brands - Worldwide Brands is a dropshipping platform that offers a directory of verified suppliers and over 16 million products from over 8,000 suppliers in various categories, including electronics, fashion, and home goods. One of its unique features is its emphasis on working directly with suppliers to ensure that they meet certain quality standards and have a good reputation in the industry. Additionally, Worldwide Brands provides various tools and resources to help merchants find and import products, including market research tools, product sourcing guides, and a community forum.

11. AliDropship - AliDropship is a unique dropshipping platform that offers a variety of services to help merchants start and grow their business. One of its main features is its custom store creation service, which provides merchants with a fully optimized dropshipping store that is ready to use out of the box. AliDropship also offers a range of tools to help merchants find and import

products from AliExpress, including a built-in product importer and automated order fulfillment. Additionally, it provides various features such as pricing automation, SEO optimization, and social media integrations to help merchants grow their business.

12. Dropship Direct - Dropship Direct is a dropshipping platform that offers a range of products, including electronics, fashion, and home goods, from its network of suppliers. One of its unique features is its integration with various eCommerce platforms, including Shopify, Magento, and eBay. Additionally, Dropship Direct provides various features such as real-time inventory updates, order tracking, and product data feeds to help merchants manage their dropshipping business more efficiently.

13. Wholesale Central - Wholesale Central is a directory of wholesalers and dropshippers that offers over 1,400 categories of products, including electronics, fashion, and home goods. One of its unique features is its emphasis on connecting merchants with US-based suppliers, which can help reduce shipping times and costs for merchants based in the US. Additionally, Wholesale Central provides various tools and resources to help merchants find and import products, including a product sourcing tool and a directory of suppliers.

14. Wholesale Hub - Wholesale Hub is a dropshipping platform that connects merchants with a network of suppliers and manufacturers that offer a range of products, including electronics, fashion, and home goods. One of its unique features is its focus on supporting small and medium-sized businesses by providing access to high-quality products at competitive prices. Additionally, Wholesale Hub provides various features such as real-time inventory updates, order tracking, and product data feeds to help merchants manage their dropshipping business more efficiently. Wholesale Hub's focus on supporting small and medium-sized businesses and its range of products make it an attractive option for merchants who want to start dropshipping without the need for a large investment in inventory.

15. Sunrise Wholesale - Sunrise Wholesale is a dropshipping platform that offers a range of products, including electronics, fashion, and

home goods, from its network of suppliers. One of its unique features is its focus on providing merchants with a comprehensive set of tools and resources to help them grow their business, including product research tools, marketing materials, and access to a community forum. Additionally, Sunrise Wholesale provides various features such as real-time inventory updates, order tracking, and customized branding options to help merchants manage their dropshipping business more efficiently. Sunrise Wholesale's focus on providing merchants with a comprehensive set of tools and resources and its range of products make it an attractive option for merchants who want to start dropshipping or grow their existing dropshipping business.

16. National Dropshippers - National Dropshippers is a dropshipping platform that offers a range of products, including electronics, fashion, and home goods, from its network of suppliers. One of its unique features is its focus on providing merchants with high-quality products from trusted suppliers at competitive prices. They provide various features such as real-time inventory updates, order tracking, and customized branding options to help merchants manage their dropshipping business more efficiently. Their focus on high-quality products and competitive prices makes it an attractive option for merchants who want a reliable and trustworthy source of products. Its low minimum order requirements and integration with popular eCommerce platforms such as Shopify and eBay also make it accessible to merchants of all sizes.

17. Megagoods - Megagoods is a dropshipping platform that offers a range of products, including electronics, fashion, and home goods, from its network of suppliers. One of its unique features is its focus on providing merchants with access to name-brand products from trusted manufacturers at competitive prices. Additionally, Megagoods provides various features such as real-time inventory updates, order tracking, and customized branding options to help merchants manage their dropshipping business more efficiently.

18. Wholesale Deals - Wholesale Deals is a dropshipping platform that offers a range of products, including electronics, fashion, and home goods, from its network of suppliers. One of its unique features is

its focus on providing merchants with access to exclusive deals and offers on products from its network of suppliers. Additionally, Wholesale Deals provides various features such as real-time inventory updates, order tracking, and customized branding options to help merchants manage their dropshipping business more efficiently.

19. Wholesale Accessory Market - Wholesale Accessory Market is a dropshipping platform that offers a range of fashion and home goods products from its network of suppliers. One of its unique features is its focus on providing merchants with access to a wide range of fashion accessories, including jewelry, handbags, and hats, from its network of suppliers. Additionally, Wholesale Accessory Market provides various features such as real-time inventory updates, order tracking, and customized branding options to help merchants manage their dropshipping business more efficiently.

20. Inventory Source - Inventory Source is a dropshipping platform that offers a range of products, including electronics, fashion, and home goods, from its network of suppliers. One of its unique features is its focus on providing merchants with a comprehensive suite of tools to manage their dropshipping business more efficiently. These tools include real-time inventory updates, order management, automated product listing, and customized branding options.

Selecting the proper platform or marketplace for your business is crucial for success. Take the time to research and evaluate the various options available, considering factors such as fees, user interface, customer reach, and integration capabilities. Consider starting with a smaller platform or marketplace and gradually expanding to larger ones as your business grows. Don't be afraid to experiment and pivot if necessary to find the best fit for your business. With the right platform or marketplace, you can reach a wider audience, increase sales, and ultimately achieve your business goals.

Chapter 2

Researching And Selecting a Niche

One of the most important steps in starting a dropshipping business is selecting the right niche. Choosing a niche that you're passionate about and that has a market demand can make all the difference in the success of your business. In this chapter, we'll explore how to research and select a niche.

1. Identify Your Interests and Passions: The first step in selecting a niche is to identify your interests and passions. It's important to choose a niche that you're passionate about because it will keep you motivated and engaged in your business. Think about your hobbies, interests, and things you enjoy doing in your free time.

2. Research Market Demand: Once you've identified your interests and passions, it's time to research market demand. Look for niches that have a large and growing market demand. You can use tools like Google Trends and Amazon Best Sellers to identify popular niches.

3. Analyze Competition: After you've identified a few potential niches, it's important to analyze the competition. Look for niches that have low competition or that you can differentiate yourself from the competition. You can use tools like Google Keyword Planner and SEMrush to analyze competition.

4. Consider Profitability: It's important to consider the profitability of a niche before selecting it. Look for niches that have high profit margins and low overhead costs. Consider factors like shipping costs, supplier pricing, and marketing costs.

5. Test and Validate: Once you've selected a niche, it's important to test and validate it. Start with a small number of products and test them in the market. Get feedback from customers and adjust as needed. Once you've validated the niche, you can scale up your business.

By identifying your interests and passions, researching market demand, analyzing competition, considering profitability, and testing and validating, you can select a niche that's right for you and your business. Based on the current market research, here are the Top 20 most popular dropshipping niches and their description:

1. Fashion and Accessories - This niche includes clothing, shoes, jewelry, and other fashion accessories.
2. Beauty and Personal Care - This niche includes skincare products, makeup, hair care products, and personal grooming tools.
3. Home and Garden - This niche includes furniture, home decor, kitchenware, and outdoor living products.
4. Electronics - This niche includes smartphones, laptops, gaming consoles, and other electronic devices.
5. Pet Supplies - This niche includes pet food, toys, beds, and other pet-related products.
6. Baby Products - This niche includes baby clothing, toys, strollers, and other baby-related products.
7. Health and Wellness - This niche includes vitamins, supplements, fitness equipment, and other health-related products.
8. Sports and Outdoors - This niche includes camping gear, hiking equipment, and other outdoor recreation products.
9. Toys and Games - This niche includes board games, puzzles, and other toys and games for children and adults.
10. Automotive - This niche includes car accessories, car care products, and other automotive-related products.
11. Home Improvement - This niche includes tools, hardware, and supplies for DIY projects and home renovations.
12. Travel and Luggage - This niche includes travel accessories, luggage, and backpacks.
13. Office Supplies - This niche includes office equipment, stationery, and other office-related products.
14. Art and Crafts - This niche includes art supplies, craft kits, and other creative products.
15. Food and Beverage - This niche includes snacks, beverages, and other food products.
16. Jewelry - This niche includes necklaces, bracelets, earrings, and other jewelry items.

17. Novelty Items - This niche includes unique and quirky products that appeal to a wide range of customers.
18. Education and Learning - This niche includes educational toys, books, and other learning materials for children and adults.
19. Phone Accessories - This niche includes cases, chargers, and other accessories for smartphones.
20. Gifts and Special Occasions - This niche includes products for special occasions such as birthdays, weddings, and holidays.

Researching and selecting a niche is a crucial step in building a successful dropshipping business. By conducting thorough market research, analyzing data and trends, and identifying gaps in the market, you can find a profitable niche that aligns with your interests and expertise. It is also important to consider factors such as competition, audience demand, and product availability when selecting a niche. With the right niche, you can differentiate yourself in a crowded marketplace and build a loyal customer base. By continuously monitoring market trends and consumer behavior, you can adapt your niche and product offerings over time to stay relevant and profitable.

Chapter 2

Finding Profitable Products to Sell

Finding profitable products to sell is one of the key factors in the success of your dropshipping business. In this chapter, we'll explore how to find profitable products to sell.

1. Analyze Market Trends: The first step in finding profitable products to sell is to analyze market trends. Look for products that are in high demand and have a growing market. You can use tools like Google Trends and Amazon Best Sellers to identify popular products.

2. Conduct Market Research: Once you've identified potential products, it's important to conduct market research. Look for products that have low competition or that you can differentiate yourself from the competition. You can use tools like Google Keyword Planner and SEMrush to analyze competition.

3. Evaluate Profit Margins: It's important to evaluate the profit margins of potential products before adding them to your store. Look for products that have high profit margins and low overhead costs. Consider factors like shipping costs, supplier pricing, and marketing costs.

4. Test and Validate: Once you've selected potential products, it's important to test and validate them. Start with a small number of products and test them in the market. Get feedback from customers and adjust as needed. Once you've validated the products, you can scale up your business.

5. Use Dropshipping Marketplaces: Dropshipping marketplaces like AliExpress, Oberlo, and SaleHoo can be a great resource for finding profitable products. These marketplaces have a wide selection of products and suppliers that have been vetted for quality.

6. Consider White Labeling: White labeling involves adding your own branding and packaging to a product that's already being produced by a manufacturer. This can help you differentiate yourself from the competition and increase your profit margins.

By analyzing market trends, conducting market research, evaluating profit margins, testing, and validating, using dropshipping marketplaces, and considering white labeling, you can find products that will be successful in your business. Here are 10 examples of high-profit margin items for dropshipping in 2023. A full list of top 10 high profit items per top performing niche will be made available in the final chapter.

1. Bluetooth Earbuds
2. Smartwatch with Fitness Tracker
3. Portable Air Conditioner
4. Electric Massager
5. Teeth Whitening Kit
6. Hair Removal Device
7. Organic Beard Oil
8. Magnetic Phone Car Mount
9. Waterproof Phone Case
10. HD Action Camera

Finding profitable products to sell is a crucial step in the success of any business. By conducting thorough market research, utilizing data and analytics, and keeping an eye on current and future trends, you can identify in-demand products that have the potential to generate high profits. Additionally, understanding your target audience and their needs and preferences can help you select products that will appeal to them and drive sales. By combining these strategies and taking the time to carefully select your products, you can set yourself up for success and achieve long-term profitability.

Chapter 3: Sourcing Your Products

Chapter 3

Overview of Different Sourcing Options
(Domestic vs. International, Wholesale vs. Retail)

When it comes to sourcing products for your business, there are several options available. Two of the primary considerations are whether to source domestically or internationally, and whether to purchase from a wholesaler or a retailer. Each option has its own advantages and disadvantages, and the choice will ultimately depend on your specific needs and goals.

Domestic Sourcing vs. International Sourcing

Domestic sourcing involves purchasing goods from suppliers within the same country as your business. This option has several advantages. For one, it can often be easier to communicate with domestic suppliers and manage the supply chain logistics. Additionally, domestic sourcing can help to support local businesses and economies.

On the other hand, international sourcing involves purchasing goods from suppliers in other countries. This option can be advantageous for several reasons. For one, it can often be more cost-effective to source internationally, as labor and production costs may be lower in other countries. Additionally, international sourcing can provide access to unique products or materials that may not be available domestically.

Wholesale Sourcing vs. Retail Sourcing

When sourcing products, another consideration is whether to purchase from a wholesaler or a retailer. Wholesale sourcing involves purchasing goods in large quantities directly from the manufacturer or a distributor. This option can be advantageous for a few reasons. For one, it can often be more cost-effective to purchase in bulk. Additionally, wholesale sourcing can provide access to a wider range of products.

Retail sourcing, on the other hand, involves purchasing goods from a retailer, who has already purchased the goods from a wholesaler or directly from the manufacturer. This option can be advantageous for businesses that do not have the resources to purchase in bulk, or that require a more flexible supply chain. Additionally, retail sourcing can provide access to products that may not be available through wholesale channels.

When considering sourcing options for your business, there are numerous factors to consider, including whether to source domestically or internationally, and whether to purchase from a wholesaler or a retailer. Ultimately, the choice will depend on your specific needs and goals. Consider the advantages and disadvantages of each option and weigh the costs and benefits carefully before deciding.

Chapter 3

Pros and Cons of Each Sourcing Option

When debating the different sourcing options, you should weigh the benefits and drawbacks of each option based on your specific business needs and goals. Domestic sourcing may be beneficial for businesses that prioritize faster shipping, better communication, and supporting the local economy. International sourcing may be beneficial for businesses that prioritize lower cost, access to unique products, and diversification of the supply chain. Wholesale sourcing may be beneficial for businesses that prioritize lower cost, a wider range of products, and stronger relationships with suppliers. Retail sourcing may be beneficial for businesses that prioritize flexibility, convenience, and no minimum order quantities.

Domestic Sourcing Pros:

1. Faster shipping and delivery.
2. Better communication with suppliers.
3. Supporting local businesses and economy.
4. Easier to ensure product quality and safety compliance.

Domestic Sourcing Cons:

1. Products may be more expensive compared to international sourcing.
2. Limited access to unique products and materials.
3. Limited options for scale and expansion.

International Sourcing Pros:

1. Lower cost of products.
2. Access to unique products and materials.
3. Diversification of supply chain.
4. Opportunity for business expansion.

International Sourcing Cons:

1. Longer shipping times and higher shipping costs.
2. Customs, import fees and taxes.

3. Language barriers and time-zone differences can hinder communication and lead to misunderstandings.
4. Quality control and safety compliance may be more challenging to monitor.

Wholesale Sourcing Pros:

1. Lower cost due to bulk purchasing.
2. Access to a wider range of products.
3. Stronger relationships with suppliers.
4. Ability to negotiate better pricing and terms.

Wholesale Sourcing Cons:

1. High minimum order quantities.
2. Limited flexibility in product customization and branding.
3. Storage and inventory management can be challenging.

Retail Sourcing Pros:

1. No minimum order quantities.
2. Flexibility in product customization and branding.
3. Convenient ordering on an as-needed basis.
4. More accessible to smaller businesses.

Retail Sourcing Cons:

1. Higher cost compared to wholesale sourcing.
2. Limited product availability and selection.
3. Limited control over product quality and safety compliance.

Ultimately, each sourcing option has its own benefits and drawbacks, and it is up to the business owner to determine which option best suits their needs and goals. Factors to consider when choosing a sourcing option include product availability, cost, speed of delivery, communication with suppliers, and quality control and safety compliance.

Chapter 3

Tips For Finding Reliable Suppliers

Of all the factors that impact the success of your business, finding reliable suppliers is one of the most crucial. Choosing the right suppliers can ensure that you have access to quality products at a reasonable price and can help you maintain a consistent supply chain. Here are some tips for finding reliable suppliers:

1. Conduct thorough research: Before signing on with a supplier, it's important to do your due diligence. This includes researching their reputation, reading reviews from other customers, and checking their background and history. Look for any red flags, such as negative reviews or lawsuits.

2. Request samples: Before committing to a supplier, it's a good idea to request samples of their products to ensure that they meet your quality standards. This will also give you an opportunity to evaluate their customer service and response time.

3. Evaluate communication: Communication is key to any successful business relationship. Evaluate how responsive the supplier is to your inquiries, how easy they are to reach, and how well they communicate in a language you are comfortable with. Look for suppliers who are willing to collaborate with you to achieve your goals.

4. Check certifications and compliance: Make sure that the supplier has all necessary certifications and complies with all regulations and standards relevant to your industry. This can include things like quality control measures, environmental regulations, and labor practices.

5. Evaluate pricing and terms: While cost is important, it shouldn't be the only factor in your decision. Look for suppliers who offer transparent pricing, reasonable payment terms, and fair return policies. Beware of suppliers who offer prices that seem too good to be true, as they may be cutting corners or using low-quality materials.

6. Ask for referrals: Ask other businesses in your industry for referrals to reliable suppliers. This can be a great way to find suppliers who have a track record of success.
7. Visit the supplier in person: If possible, visit the supplier in person to get a better sense of their operations and how they work. This can also be a good opportunity to establish a more personal relationship with the supplier.

Finding reliable suppliers is a crucial aspect of running a successful business. By following these tips and doing your research, you can ensure that you are partnering with suppliers who will help your business thrive.

Chapter 4: Managing Your Online Store

Chapter 4

Setting Up Your Website or Storefront

In today's digital age, having an online presence is essential for any business looking to reach a wider audience and grow. Whether you're starting a new business or looking to expand an existing one, setting up a website or storefront can be a great way to increase your visibility and attract new customers. Your website is open 24/7, unlike a traditional brick and mortar store. It's also both cost effective and easier to manage than a physical presence. Here are some tips for setting up your website or storefront:

1. Determine your goals: Before setting up your website or storefront, it's important to determine your goals. Are you looking to sell products online, generate leads, or simply establish a digital presence? Your goals will dictate the features and functionality you need.

2. Choose a domain name: Your domain name is the address people will use to find your website or storefront. Choose a name that is short, memorable, and easy to spell. Consider using keywords relevant to your industry.

3. Choose a platform: There are many platforms available for setting up a website or storefront, such as Shopify, WooCommerce, and Wix. Choose a platform that suits your needs and budget, and that offers features such as secure payment processing, mobile responsiveness, and customization options.

4. Design your website or storefront: Your website or storefront should be visually appealing, easy to navigate, and reflective of your brand. Consider hiring a professional designer or using a pre-made template to ensure a polished and consistent look.

5. Write content: Your website or storefront should have clear and concise content that communicates your brand's value proposition and key messages. Use keywords relevant to your industry to improve your search engine rankings.

6. Set up payment processing: If you're selling products online, you'll need to set up payment processing. Choose a provider that is

secure and offers multiple payment options, such as credit cards and PayPal.

7. Test and launch: Before launching your website or storefront, test it thoroughly to ensure it is functioning properly and is user-friendly. Consider asking friends or family to test it as well. Once you're satisfied with the site, launch it and begin promoting it through social media, email marketing, and other channels.

Setting up your website or storefront can be a challenging process, but with careful planning and attention to detail, it can be an asset to your business. By following these tips, you can create a website or storefront that attracts and retains customers, and helps you achieve your business goals.

Chapter 4

Designing Your Website for Maximum Conversions

Having a website is not just about having an online presence. It's about converting visitors into customers. Designing your website for maximum conversions is important because it can directly impact your business's success. A conversion is when a website visitor takes a desired action, such as making a purchase, filling out a contact form, or subscribing to a newsletter. When you design your website with the goal of maximizing conversions, you're creating a website that is optimized for driving business results. Here are some tips for designing your website for maximum conversions:

1. Create a clear and concise message: Your website's message should be clear and concise. Visitors should be able to understand what your business does and what it offers within a few seconds of landing on your homepage.

2. Use compelling visuals: Use high-quality images and videos to showcase your products or services. Use visuals that are relevant to your target audience and highlight the benefits of your offerings.

3. Use a responsive design: Your website should be optimized for all devices, including desktops, tablets, and smartphones. A responsive design ensures that your website is easy to navigate and read on any device.

4. Make it easy to navigate: Your website's navigation should be intuitive and easy to use. Use clear labels for your menu items and make it easy for visitors to find what they're looking for.

5. Optimize your calls to action: Your calls to action (CTAs) should be prominent, clear, and compelling. Use action-oriented language and place your CTAs in prominent locations on your website.

6. Use social proof: Social proof can be a powerful tool for increasing conversions. Use customer reviews, testimonials, and endorsements from influencers to build trust with your visitors.

7. Offer incentives: Offer incentives such as discounts, free shipping, or a free trial to encourage visitors to act. Use these incentives strategically to encourage conversions.

8. Monitor and test: Monitor your website's performance using tools such as Google Analytics. Test different elements of your website, such as your CTAs, headlines, and visuals, to see what works best.

Designing a website for maximum conversions is crucial for the success of any business, but it is especially important for a dropshipper. Your website is the face of your business, and it is the first point of contact for your potential customers. A well-designed website with clear navigation, compelling product descriptions, high-quality images, and easy checkout processes can help increase customer engagement, build trust, and drive more sales. To achieve maximum conversions, it is important to optimize your website for both desktop and mobile users and continuously test and refine your design and content to improve the user experience. By investing time and resources into designing a website that converts, you can increase your revenue, grow your customer base, and ultimately succeed in the competitive world of dropshipping.

Chapter 4

Creating Product Descriptions That Sell

Creating product descriptions that sell is crucial for eCommerce businesses because they play a vital role in converting potential customers into actual buyers. The product description is the text that accompanies a product image and provides detailed information about the product's features, benefits, and specifications. A well-crafted product description can be the difference between a customer clicking "Add to Cart" or clicking away from your website.

Key Tips

1. Know your target audience: Before you start writing product descriptions, it's important to know your target audience. Understand their needs, desires, and pain points. Use language and tone that will resonate with them.

2. Highlight the benefits: Rather than just listing the features of your product, focus on the benefits. Explain how your product will make your customer's life better or solve a problem they're facing.

3. Use descriptive language: Use descriptive language to create a vivid picture of your product in the customer's mind. Use sensory words to describe how it looks, feels, smells, and sounds.

4. Be concise: While it's important to provide detailed information about your product, it's also important to be concise. Use short sentences and paragraphs and break up the text with bullet points.

5. Use keywords: Use keywords relevant to your product and industry to improve your search engine rankings. Use them naturally in your product descriptions.

6. Provide social proof: Provide social proof in the form of customer reviews, ratings, and testimonials. This will build trust with potential customers and persuade them to make a purchase.

7. Create a sense of urgency: Use language that creates a sense of urgency, such as limited stock or a limited-time offer. This can encourage customers to make a purchase before it's too late.

8. Use storytelling: Use storytelling to create an emotional connection with your customers. Explain the story behind your product, or how it has helped other customers in the past.

Artificial intelligence (AI) is revolutionizing the way we do business, including how we write product descriptions. AI-powered tools can help you create product descriptions that are not only informative but also persuasive. By using AI for product descriptions, you can create more persuasive, customized, and effective descriptions that sell. These AI-powered tools can help you save time, improve your SEO, and increase your sales. Here are some ways you can use AI for product descriptions that sell:

1. Generate product descriptions automatically: With the help of AI, you can generate product descriptions automatically. These descriptions can be customized based on your product and target audience and can save you time and effort.

2. Use natural language processing: Natural language processing (NLP) can help you create product descriptions that are more natural-sounding and easier to read. NLP can analyze your existing product descriptions and suggest improvements to make them more persuasive.

3. Personalize your product descriptions: AI can help you personalize your product descriptions based on each customer's browsing and purchase history. By tailoring your descriptions to each customer, you can increase the chances of making a sale.

4. Use sentiment analysis: Sentiment analysis can help you understand how customers feel about your products. By analyzing customer reviews and feedback, you can identify areas where your products excel and areas that need improvement. This can help you create more persuasive product descriptions that address customer concerns.

5. Optimize your descriptions for SEO: AI-powered tools can help you optimize your product descriptions for search engine optimization (SEO). By using relevant keywords and phrases, you can improve your search engine rankings and increase your visibility to potential customers.

6. Use chatbots: Chatbots powered by AI can provide personalized recommendations and product descriptions to customers in real-time. This can help customers find the products they're looking for more quickly and easily.
7. Improve your translations: AI can help you improve your product descriptions translations in multiple languages. AI can analyze the meaning and context of your descriptions and provide accurate translations.

Chatbots

1. Mitsuku: Created by Steve Worswick, Mitsuku has won several awards for its conversational abilities. It uses AI and natural language processing to provide personalized responses to users.
2. Replika: Replika is an AI-powered chatbot that is designed to act as a personal assistant and friend. It uses machine learning to learn about the user's preferences and interests and provides personalized responses.
3. Xiaoice: Developed by Microsoft, Xiaoice is a Chinese chatbot that has over 660 million users. It uses natural language processing, machine learning, and emotional computing to provide realistic and emotional responses.
4. Cleverbot: Cleverbot is an AI-powered chatbot that has been around since 1997. It uses machine learning to learn from its conversations with users and provide more human-like responses.
5. ChatGPT: ChatGPT is a large language model developed by OpenAI. It uses artificial intelligence to provide natural language responses to users' queries and conversations.

By following these tips, you can create product descriptions that sell. Remember to focus on the benefits, use descriptive language, and create a sense of urgency. By doing so, you can persuade potential customers to make a purchase and achieve your business goals.

Chapter 4

Tips For Optimizing Your Product Pages for Search Engines

If you have an online store, optimizing your product pages for search engines is crucial for driving organic traffic and increasing sales. It helps to improve your online visibility and attract potential customers to your website. When people search for products or services online, they usually use search engines like Google, Bing, or Yahoo. These search engines use complex algorithms to determine which web pages should appear in their search results.

Optimizing your product pages for search engines involves incorporating relevant keywords and phrases, optimizing images, ensuring mobile-friendliness and page speed, adding customer reviews and ratings, using schema markup, and creating unique and compelling product descriptions. By doing so, your product pages become more visible to search engines, which can lead to higher rankings in search results.

Higher search engine rankings can result in increased organic traffic to your website, which can ultimately lead to more sales and revenue for your business. Additionally, optimizing your product pages for search engines can help to improve the overall user experience of your website, which can lead to increased customer satisfaction and loyalty.

In today's competitive eCommerce landscape, optimizing your product pages for search engines is no longer an option, but a necessity. It can help you stand out from your competitors and ensure that your products are visible to potential customers who are actively searching for them online. Here are some tips for optimizing your product pages for search engines:

1. Conduct keyword research: Use tools like Google Keyword Planner or Ahrefs to identify the relevant keywords and phrases that your target audience is using to search for products like yours. Incorporate these keywords and phrases into your product page title, meta descriptions, headers, and body copy to improve your search engine rankings.

2. Optimize your images: Images play a vital role in eCommerce, so make sure to optimize them for search engines. Add relevant alt text descriptions to your images and compress them for faster page loading times. This can help improve your search engine rankings and ensure that your products show up in image search results.

3. Ensure mobile-friendliness and page speed: Google takes mobile-friendliness and page speed into account when ranking web pages. Therefore, it's crucial to ensure that your product pages are mobile-friendly and have a fast-loading speed. A slow-loading page can increase your bounce rate and negatively impact your SEO.

4. Include customer reviews and ratings: Adding customer reviews and ratings to your product pages provides valuable social proof for your products. It also creates fresh, user-generated content that can improve your search engine rankings.

5. Use schema markup: Schema markup provides additional information about your products to search engines. It can include information such as pricing, availability, and product reviews. Using schema markup can help improve your search engine rankings and increase the visibility of your products in search results.

6. Create unique and compelling product descriptions: Avoid duplicating content from other product pages or manufacturer descriptions. Instead, create unique and compelling product descriptions that highlight the features, benefits, and unique selling points of your products. This can help improve your search engine rankings and encourage potential customers to make a purchase.

Follow these tips for optimizing your product pages for search engines, and you can increase your online visibility, attract more potential customers, and improve your overall SEO.

Chapter 5 - Marketing Your Dropshipping Business

Chapter 5

Overview Of Different Marketing Channels
(Paid Advertising, Social Media, Email Marketing, Etc.)

Marketing channels are the various ways businesses can promote their products or services to potential customers. There are many different marketing channels available, each with its own strengths and challenges. Some of the most common marketing channels include paid advertising, social media, email marketing, content marketing, search engine optimization (SEO), and influencer marketing.

The key to effective marketing is to select the channels that are most likely to reach your target audience and align with your marketing goals, and to develop a comprehensive marketing strategy that leverages multiple channels for maximum impact. By understanding the strengths and limitations of each marketing channel, businesses can optimize their marketing efforts to connect with potential customers, build brand awareness, and drive sales and revenue growth. Here is an overview of some of the most common ones:

1. Paid advertising: This includes any form of advertising that a business pays for, such as search engine ads, display ads, social media ads, and sponsored content. Paid advertising can be highly targeted and effective, but it can also be costly.
2. Social media: Social media platforms like Facebook, Instagram, Twitter, and LinkedIn offer businesses the opportunity to connect with customers, build brand awareness, and promote products or services. Social media can be an effective way to engage with customers, but it requires ongoing effort and a solid social media strategy.
3. Email marketing: Email marketing involves sending promotional messages or newsletters to a list of subscribers. This can be an effective way to nurture leads and build customer relationships, but it requires a well-crafted email marketing strategy and a high-quality email list.

4. Content marketing: Content marketing involves creating and sharing valuable content such as blog posts, infographics, videos, and whitepapers that educate and engage potential customers. This can be an effective way to build brand awareness and establish thought leadership, but it requires a consistent content creation and distribution strategy.
5. Search engine optimization (SEO): SEO involves optimizing your website and content to rank higher in search engine results pages (SERPs) for specific keywords or phrases. This can be an effective way to drive organic traffic to your website, but it requires ongoing effort and a solid SEO strategy.
6. Influencer marketing: Influencer marketing involves partnering with influential people in your industry or niche to promote your products or services to their followers. This can be an effective way to reach a highly engaged and targeted audience, but it requires careful selection of influencers and a clear influencer marketing strategy.

In summary, there are many different marketing channels available to businesses, each with its own strengths and challenges. The key is to select the channels that are most likely to reach your target audience and align with your marketing goals, and to develop a comprehensive marketing strategy that leverages multiple channels for maximum impact.

Chapter 5

Creating A Marketing Strategy That Works for Your Business

Creating a marketing strategy for your business is important because it provides a roadmap for effectively promoting your products or services to your target audience. By identifying your ideal customer, setting marketing goals, and determining the best channels and tactics to reach them, you can optimize your marketing efforts for maximum impact and return on investment.

A well-crafted marketing strategy can help you to differentiate your business from competitors, build brand awareness and credibility, increase customer engagement and loyalty, and ultimately drive sales and revenue growth. Without a clear marketing strategy in place, your business risks wasting time and resources on ineffective marketing tactics and missing out on valuable opportunities to connect with potential customers. Here are some tips for developing a marketing strategy that works for your business:

1. Define your target audience: The first step in creating a marketing strategy is to define your target audience. This involves identifying the demographic, psychographic, and behavioral characteristics of your ideal customer. By understanding who your target audience is, you can develop messaging and promotional materials that resonate with them.

2. Set measurable goals: Once you have defined your target audience, you need to set measurable goals for your marketing efforts. This might include increasing website traffic, generating more leads, or increasing sales revenue. By setting clear and specific goals, you can measure the effectiveness of your marketing efforts and make data-driven decisions to optimize your strategy.

3. Choose the right marketing channels: There are many different marketing channels available, each with its own strengths and challenges. The key is to select the channels that are most likely to reach your target audience and align with your marketing goals. This might include paid advertising, social media, email

marketing, content marketing, search engine optimization (SEO), or influencer marketing.

4. Develop a messaging strategy: Your messaging strategy should be tailored to your target audience and aligned with your marketing goals. This might include developing a unique value proposition, crafting compelling headlines and taglines, and creating messaging that resonates with your audience's pain points and desires.

5. Create a content plan: Content is a critical component of any marketing strategy. By creating high-quality, engaging content that provides value to your target audience, you can establish thought leadership, build trust, and drive traffic to your website. This might include blog posts, infographics, videos, whitepapers, or case studies.

6. Measure and optimize: Once your marketing strategy is in place, it's important to measure and optimize your efforts. This might include tracking website analytics, monitoring social media engagement, or conducting A/B testing on ad copy or landing pages. By making data-driven decisions and continually optimizing your strategy, you can improve your ROI and achieve your marketing goals.

In summary, creating a marketing strategy that works for your business requires careful planning, research, and ongoing optimization. By defining your target audience, setting measurable goals, selecting the right marketing channels, developing a messaging strategy, creating high-quality content, and measuring and optimizing your efforts, you can build a successful marketing program that drives growth and revenue for your business.

Chapter 5

Tips for Optimizing Your Advertising Campaigns for Maximum ROI

Optimizing your advertising campaign for maximum ROI is crucial because it helps you to make the most of your advertising budget and achieve your marketing goals. By continually refining and improving your campaigns, you can ensure that you are targeting the right audience, using the most effective channels, and delivering the most compelling ad messaging. This can help you to increase conversions, drive sales, and maximize your revenue, all while minimizing your advertising spend.

By optimizing your campaigns for maximum ROI, you can achieve a better return on investment for your marketing efforts, allowing you to allocate resources more effectively and achieve your business objectives more efficiently. Here are some tips for optimizing your advertising campaigns:

1. Define your target audience: The more you know about your target audience, the more effectively you can craft your advertising messages and select the right channels to reach them. Consider demographic, psychographic, and behavioral characteristics when defining your audience.
2. Use the right channels: There are many different advertising channels available, from search engine marketing to social media ads to display advertising. Choose the channels that are most likely to reach your target audience and align with your marketing goals.
3. Set clear goals: Set specific, measurable goals for your advertising campaigns, such as increasing website traffic, generating leads, or driving sales. Use these goals to guide your campaign development and evaluate its effectiveness.
4. Craft compelling ad copy: Your ad copy should be concise, clear, and compelling. Use attention-grabbing headlines and strong calls to action to encourage clicks and conversions.
5. Optimize your landing pages: Your landing pages should be optimized to convert visitors into leads or customers. Use clear,

concise messaging, compelling images, and strong calls to action to encourage visitors to act.

6. Monitor and adjust: Continually monitor your campaigns and adjust your strategies as needed. Use data to evaluate your campaign's effectiveness and make data-driven decisions to optimize your advertising efforts.

7. Test and iterate: A/B testing is a powerful way to optimize your advertising campaigns. Test different ad copy, landing pages, and calls to action to identify what works best for your audience and improve your campaign's ROI over time.

By following these tips and continually optimizing your advertising campaigns, you can maximize your ROI and drive growth and revenue for your business.

Chapter 6: Managing Your Finances and Logistics

Chapter 6

Understanding Profit Margins and Pricing Strategies

Understanding profit margins and pricing strategies is essential for any business that wants to be successful in the long run. Profit margin is the difference between the cost of producing a product or service and the revenue generated from selling it. A pricing strategy, on the other hand, is a plan for determining the optimal price to charge for a product or service to maximize profits.

There are several pricing strategies to consider, including cost-plus pricing, value-based pricing, penetration pricing, and skimming pricing. Cost-plus pricing involves adding a markup to the cost of producing a product or service to arrive at the selling price. Value-based pricing, on the other hand, focuses on setting prices based on the perceived value of the product or service to the customer. Penetration pricing involves setting a low initial price to attract customers and gain market share, while skimming pricing involves setting a high initial price to maximize profits from early adopters. Here are some of the pros and cons of each:

Cost-Plus Pricing Pros

1. Easy to calculate: By simply adding a markup to the cost of production, businesses can arrive at the selling price.
2. Ensures profitability: Cost-plus pricing ensures that a business makes a profit on each product or service sold.

Cost-Plus Pricing Cons

1. Ignores customer demand: Cost-plus pricing does not consider what customers are willing to pay for a product or service.
2. May not be competitive: If competitors are using value-based pricing or other strategies to set lower prices, cost-plus pricing may not be competitive.

Value-Based Pricing Pros

1. Considers customer demand: Value-based pricing considers what customers are willing to pay for a product or service based on the perceived value.
2. Can lead to higher profits: By setting prices higher than cost-plus pricing, value-based pricing can lead to higher profits.

Value-Based Pricing Cons

1. Difficult to determine: It can be challenging to accurately determine the perceived value of a product or service.
2. May not be competitive: If competitors are using cost-plus pricing or other strategies to set lower prices, value-based pricing may not be competitive.

Penetration Pricing Pros

1. Attracts customers: By setting a low initial price, penetration pricing can attract new customers and gain market share.
2. Can lead to higher profits: Once a customer base is established, prices can be increased to maximize profits.

Penetration Pricing Cons

1. May not be profitable: If prices are too low, the business may not make enough profit to sustain operations.
2. Can lead to price sensitivity: Once prices are raised, customers may become sensitive to price and be less willing to pay more.

Skimming Pricing Pros

1. Can lead to higher profits: By setting a high initial price, skimming pricing can maximize profits from early adopters.
2. Creates an image of exclusivity: High prices can create an image of exclusivity and luxury.

Skimming Pricing Cons

1. May not be sustainable: Once early adopters have purchased the product, sales may decline if prices are not adjusted.

2. May not be competitive: Competitors may use lower pricing strategies to attract customers and gain market share.

When determining pricing strategies, it is important to consider factors such as production costs, competition, customer demand, and market trends. In addition, understanding profit margins is crucial to make informed decisions about pricing and ensure that the business is sustainable and profitable over time.

Ultimately, a successful pricing strategy should not only generate revenue but also consider the cost of production and other expenses to ensure a healthy profit margin. By carefully analyzing costs, competition, and customer demand, businesses can set pricing strategies that balance revenue and profitability to achieve long-term success.

Chapter 6

Managing Your Inventory & Orders

Managing inventory and orders can be a complex task for any business, particularly for those that operate with dropshipping. Dropshipping is a business model in which the retailer does not keep inventory in stock but instead forwards the customer orders and shipment details to the manufacturer or supplier, who then fulfills the orders directly to the customer.

Managing inventory and orders with dropshipping can have its benefits and challenges. Here are some tips to help you manage your inventory and orders effectively:

1. Choose reliable suppliers: When dropshipping, your suppliers are responsible for fulfilling the orders, so it is essential to work with reliable and trustworthy suppliers. Do thorough research and evaluate the supplier's reputation and track record before partnering with them.

2. Keep track of inventory levels: Even though you do not have to physically hold inventory with dropshipping, it is still essential to keep track of the inventory levels of your suppliers. This can help you avoid selling products that are out of stock.

3. Automate order processing: Automating order processing can help streamline the dropshipping process and save time. Consider using tools and software that can automatically forward orders and shipment details to your suppliers. Oberlo, ShipStation, Dropified, Printful, and Inventory Source are some to research and see if they're right for you.

4. Monitor order fulfillment: Keep an eye on order fulfillment to ensure that your customers receive their orders on time. Communicate regularly with your suppliers to confirm shipment details and any potential delays.

5. Providing excellent customer service can help build trust and loyalty with your customers.

Managing inventory and orders with dropshipping requires a different approach than traditional inventory management. By choosing reliable suppliers, automating order processing, and monitoring order fulfillment, you can successfully manage your business and ensure customer satisfaction.

Chapter 6

Handling Returns and Customer Service Issues

Handling returns and customer service issues can be a bit tricky for dropshipping businesses as they do not have direct control over the inventory and shipping process. However, with proper planning and communication with suppliers, it is possible to manage these issues efficiently.

Key Tips

1. Have clear return policies: Make sure to have a clear and detailed return policy on your website to avoid confusion and misunderstandings with customers. Communicate the return policy to customers before they make a purchase and ensure that it aligns with the policies of your suppliers.

2. Communicate with suppliers: Establish clear communication channels with your suppliers to ensure that they are aware of your return policies and procedures. Communicate with them regularly to stay updated on inventory levels, shipping times, and other relevant information.

3. Train customer service staff: Make sure that your customer service staff is well-trained and equipped to handle customer inquiries and complaints. They should have a clear understanding of your return policies and be able to communicate them effectively to customers.

4. Offer excellent customer service: Providing excellent customer service can go a long way in building customer loyalty and increasing sales. Respond promptly to customer inquiries and complaints and do your best to resolve issues in a timely and satisfactory manner.

5. Consider offering incentives: Offering incentives such as free returns or exchanges can help attract and retain customers. Consider offering these incentives to customers who experience issues with their orders or returns.

6. Use automation tools: Consider using automation tools such as chatbots and help desk software to streamline customer service processes and improve response times.

Handling returns and customer service issues with dropshipping requires careful planning and communication with suppliers. By having clear policies and procedures in place and offering excellent customer service, businesses can effectively manage these issues and build customer loyalty.

Chapter 6

Tips For Streamlining Your Logistics & Fulfillment Process

Dropshipping is a popular fulfillment method for ecommerce businesses because it allows for a streamlined logistics and fulfillment process. Streamlining your logistics and fulfillment process with dropshipping is important for several reasons. It can save you time, reduce costs, improve efficiency, and it can scale with your business. Here are some tips for optimizing this process:

1. Choose reliable suppliers: Before partnering with a dropshipping supplier, make sure to research their reputation and reliability. Working with reputable suppliers can help ensure timely and accurate order fulfillment.

2. Automate your order processing: Many dropshipping platforms offer tools for automating order processing, such as automatically sending tracking information to customers. Automating this process can save time and reduce errors.

3. Use efficient packaging and shipping methods: Choosing the right packaging and shipping methods can help streamline your logistics process. For example, using lightweight packaging can reduce shipping costs, while using a fulfillment center with multiple locations can speed up delivery times.

4. Implement quality control measures: While dropshipping can streamline fulfillment, it's still important to ensure the quality of your products. Implement quality control measures, such as inspecting products before they're shipped to customers, to prevent issues with returns and customer service.

5. Utilize analytics to optimize your process: Keep track of metrics such as shipping times, order accuracy, and customer satisfaction to identify areas for improvement in your logistics and fulfillment process. Use this data to make informed decisions about your suppliers, packaging and shipping methods, and quality control measures. Shipstation, Shopify Analytics and Metrilo and some of the more popular software to help you with your analysis.

6. Overall, streamlining your logistics and fulfillment process with dropshipping can help you run a more efficient and cost-effective business, while also providing a better customer experience.

Streamlining your logistics and fulfillment process is essential for the success of your dropshipping business. By optimizing your shipping, inventory management, and order fulfillment processes, you can reduce costs, improve efficiency, and enhance customer satisfaction.

Remember to focus on choosing the right shipping partners, automating your inventory management, and regularly reviewing your processes to identify areas for improvement. With these tips, you can streamline your logistics and fulfillment processes and set your business up for long-term success.

Chapter 7: Scaling Your Business

Chapter 7

How To Grow Your Business & Increase Profits

One of the most important skills needed to grow a business and increase profits is marketing. Dropshipping is no different. Having a solid understanding of marketing strategies, such as social media advertising, search engine optimization, and email marketing, can help you reach a larger audience and drive more sales.

Having strong customer service skills can help you retain customers and build a positive reputation for your brand, which can lead to repeat business and referrals. It's also important to have good financial management skills to ensure that your profits are being maximized and your expenses are being minimized.

Growing your business and increasing profits with dropshipping requires a combination of strategies and tactics to attract more customers, increase sales, and optimize your operations. Here are some tips to help you achieve these goals:

1. Expand your product line: As you gain experience and knowledge about your niche, consider adding new products to your inventory. This will increase your potential customer base and help you stand out from competitors.

2. Use social media and content marketing: Build your brand and engage with customers through social media and content marketing. This includes creating high-quality blog posts, videos, and social media posts that educate, inform, and entertain your audience.

3. Focus on customer service: Provide excellent customer service to ensure repeat business and positive reviews. Respond promptly to inquiries and issues and go above and beyond to exceed customer expectations.

4. Offer promotions and discounts: Run special promotions and discounts to attract new customers and incentivize existing customers to make repeat purchases.

5. Optimize your website for conversions: Continuously test and optimize your website to improve the user experience and increase conversion rates. This includes optimizing your product pages, checkout process, and overall website design.

6. Implement email marketing campaigns: Use email marketing to stay in touch with customers, promote new products and promotions, and offer exclusive discounts.

7. Explore new sales channels: Consider expanding your sales channels beyond your website, such as selling on marketplaces like Amazon or eBay, or using social media platforms to sell directly to customers.

8. Analyze and optimize your metrics: Regularly review and analyze your metrics, such as traffic, conversion rates, and order values, to identify areas for improvement and make data-driven decisions.

To achieve growth and profitability with your business, it's crucial to implement the right strategies and continuously improve your operations. Building a successful enterprise requires a blend of marketing knowledge, excellent customer service, and financial know-how. Applying these skills can help you expand your reach, retain customers, reduce costs, and increase your bottom line. By carefully monitoring these elements and making necessary adjustments, you can build a thriving business and achieve long-term success.

Chapter 7

Expanding Your Product Offerings & Niches

Expanding your product offerings and niches is a crucial step to grow your dropshipping business and increase profits. While starting with a niche product or category may have been a smart move initially, diversifying your product offerings can open new opportunities for revenue streams.

One way to expand your product offerings is to conduct market research to identify products or categories that are in high demand but have low competition. You can also consider complementary products that can be sold together with your existing offerings to increase order values. Here are some steps to conduct market research:

1. Identify your target audience: Determine who your target customers are, what their needs and preferences are, and what products they are interested in.
2. Analyze the competition: Look at the websites and social media profiles of your competitors to see what products they offer, their pricing strategies, and their unique selling propositions (USPs).
3. Keyword research: Use keyword research tools to find out what people are searching for online related to your niche. This can give you an idea of what products are in demand.
4. Check social media trends: Look at social media platforms like Facebook, Instagram, and Twitter to see what products are trending in your niche.
5. Attend trade shows: Attend trade shows and events related to your niche to see what new products are being introduced, what the latest trends are, and to network with suppliers and other industry professionals.
6. Ask your customers: Ask your existing customers what products they would like to see in your store or what niches they are interested in.

Another approach is to consider expanding into a new niche altogether. This requires research and understanding of the new niche's market, target audience, and potential suppliers. Consider the cost and profitability of selling in this new niche and whether it aligns with your current business goals and operations. There are several ways to find new niches to expand your dropshipping business into:

1. Keyword research: Use tools like Google Keyword Planner, Ubersuggest, or Ahrefs to identify keywords that are popular and relevant to your existing products. Look for related keywords and topics that may suggest new niches.

2. Competitor research: Analyze your competitors' websites, social media accounts, and product offerings to identify any gaps or areas where you can differentiate yourself. Look for niches that are underserved or overlooked by your competitors.

3. Customer feedback: Pay attention to feedback from your customers, including comments, reviews, and emails. Look for recurring themes or requests that may suggest new niches or products to offer.

4. Trend analysis: Stay current on the latest trends in your industry or related industries. Look for emerging trends or changes in consumer behavior that may suggest new niches.

5. Online communities: Join online communities related to your industry or niche, such as forums, Facebook groups, or Reddit communities. Pay attention to the conversations and topics that come up frequently and look for opportunities to fill gaps or offer solutions.

Leveraging data and analytics can help you identify which products are selling well and which ones are not. Data and analytics can be useful in identifying potential niches and products to add to your business. Begin by examining your current customer base and looking for patterns in their purchasing behavior, such as the types of products they are buying or the demographics they belong to. This can provide insight into what products or niches may be worth exploring.

Use tools like Google Trends or keyword research tools to identify popular search terms and topics related to your current offerings. This can help you identify potential niches that may be worth exploring further.

Consider using data analysis tools to track your website traffic and sales patterns. Look for areas where you may be losing customers, such as high cart abandonment rates, and consider adding products or niches that could help address these issues.

Overall, expanding your product offerings and niches can lead to new revenue streams and increased profitability for your business. However, it's important to approach it strategically and with careful consideration of the market, competition, and your overall business goals.

Chapter 7

Tips for Outsourcing Tasks to Free Up Your Time

Outsourcing tasks can be a great way to free up your time and increase productivity in your business. There are only so many hours in the day and it's important to use them wisely. By outsourcing tasks, you can focus on the core functions of your business, such as developing new products, building customer relationships, and growing your brand. Additionally, outsourcing can provide access to specialized skills or knowledge that you may not have within your organization, allowing you to complete tasks more efficiently and effectively.

By delegating tasks to others, you can also reduce your workload and prevent burnout, leading to a healthier work-life balance. Ultimately, outsourcing can help you save time, increase productivity, and improve the overall success of your business. Here are some tips to help you successfully outsource tasks:

1. Determine which tasks to outsource: First, identify which tasks are taking up too much of your time and which tasks you're not skilled in. These are the tasks that you should consider outsourcing.
2. Find the right people: Look for reliable and competent freelancers or agencies that have experience in the task you need to be completed. Platforms such as Upwork, Fiverr, and Freelancer can be a good starting point.
3. Clearly communicate your expectations: Provide detailed instructions and clear deadlines to your outsourced team to ensure they understand the task's requirements.
4. Check in regularly: Regular communication with your outsourced team can help prevent any miscommunications or misunderstandings. Make sure to schedule regular check-ins to stay updated on the progress of the tasks.
5. Set up a system for feedback and improvement: Constructive feedback can help your outsourced team improve their performance and work better for you. Establish a system for providing feedback and improvement suggestions.

6. Document and track progress: Maintain a record of all outsourced work, including timelines, expenses, and results. This can help you identify areas for improvement and inform future outsourcing decisions.

7. Consider automation: Automating certain tasks can reduce the need for outsourcing, freeing up even more of your time. For instance, using social media scheduling tools like Hootsuite or Buffer can eliminate the need for a social media manager.

By outsourcing tasks, you can free up your time to focus on the more important aspects of your business. Use these tips to ensure a successful outsourcing experience and ultimately boost your productivity and profitability.

Chapter 7

Future Trends and Predictions

The dropshipping industry has experienced significant growth over the past few years, thanks in part to advancements in technology, globalization, and changing consumer behavior. As the industry continues to evolve, it's essential to keep an eye on future trends and predictions to stay ahead of the curve.

Keeping an eye out for future trends and predictions is crucial in any industry, including dropshipping. It allows businesses to stay ahead of the curve and adapt to new changes and challenges. By anticipating changes in consumer behavior, technology, and other factors, businesses can prepare for the future and make strategic decisions that will keep them competitive.

In the fast-paced world of dropshipping, trends and predictions can have a significant impact on business success. For example, changes in popular social media platforms or changes in shipping regulations can greatly affect a business's bottom line. By staying informed about trends and predictions, businesses can pivot their strategies and adapt to new circumstances, making them more likely to succeed.

Keeping an eye on future trends and predictions can also help businesses identify new opportunities for growth and expansion. For example, emerging markets or new products may offer untapped potential for revenue and profit. By being proactive and taking advantage of these opportunities, businesses can set themselves apart from their competitors and establish themselves as industry leaders. Here are some essential keys & insights to prepare yourself for an evolving market:

1. Increased focus on sustainability and ethical practices: In recent years, consumers have become more conscious about the impact of their purchases on the environment and society. As a result, there is a growing demand for products that are sustainably produced and ethically sourced. Business owners who can offer these types

of products and demonstrate their commitment to sustainability and ethical practices are likely to be successful.

2. The rise of micro-niches: As the market becomes more crowded, dropshippers are increasingly focusing on narrow product niches to stand out from the competition. These micro-niches can include products that cater to specific interests, hobbies, or lifestyles. By focusing on a specific niche, dropshippers can better understand their target audience and deliver a more personalized experience.

3. Integration with social media: Social media platforms like Instagram, Facebook, and Pinterest have become popular channels for discovering new products and brands. As a result, dropshippers are increasingly using these platforms to drive traffic and sales to their online stores. Expect to see more integration between platforms and social media in the future, allowing for easier product promotion and a more seamless shopping experience.

4. Expansion of global sourcing: With the rise of globalization, it's becoming easier for people to source products from around the world. This expansion of global sourcing is likely to continue, allowing people to find unique and innovative products to offer their customers.

5. Increased automation and AI: Automation and artificial intelligence are transforming the way businesses operate, and the dropshipping industry is no exception. Expect to see more entrepreneurs using AI and automation tools to optimize their operations, such as automatic order processing, inventory management, and customer service.

6. Diversification of sales channels: As the industry becomes more competitive, dropshippers are exploring different sales channels to reach their target audience. Expect to see more entrepreneurs selling on marketplaces like Amazon and eBay, in addition to their own online stores. Some may also explore brick-and-mortar retail options to expand their reach.

7. Increased emphasis on customer experience: As the industry continues to mature, the customer experience will become even more critical. Dropshippers who prioritize customer service and

offer a seamless shopping experience are likely to see higher customer retention rates and increased sales.

Overall, staying informed about future trends and predictions is a key component of a successful strategy. By anticipating changes and opportunities, businesses can stay competitive, grow their revenue, and achieve long-term success. By embracing new technologies, focusing on sustainability and ethical practices, and delivering a personalized customer experience, entrepreneurs can stay ahead of the curve and thrive in a competitive market.

Chapter 8: Legal Considerations

Chapter 8

Overview of Legal Considerations

When starting a dropshipping business, it's essential to understand the legal considerations involved to protect your business and avoid any legal problems down the line.

The first step in starting any business is registering it with the appropriate government agencies. Depending on your location and the size of your business, you may need to obtain a business license or permit, register for sales tax or VAT, or register your business with other regulatory bodies. Make sure you research the specific requirements in your location and comply with all necessary regulations to avoid any legal issues.

As a business owner, you'll be responsible for paying taxes on your profits. In addition to sales tax or VAT, you may also need to pay income tax and other taxes depending on your location and the nature of your business. Make sure you understand your tax obligations and keep accurate financial records to make tax season less stressful.

When selling products online, it's important to have clear policies and terms of service that outline your business practices and protect your customers. These policies should include information on your return and refund policy, shipping times and fees, and any other important information that customers should know. Additionally, it's important to include disclaimers and legal notices to protect your business from any liability.

When selecting products to sell, it's essential to ensure that you're not infringing on anyone else's intellectual property rights. This includes trademarks, patents, and copyrights. Make sure you research the products you're considering selling and avoid any products that could potentially infringe on someone else's intellectual property. Additionally, it's important to protect your own intellectual property rights by trademarking your business name, logo, and any other unique branding elements.

Understanding the legal considerations involved in starting and running a dropshipping business is essential to protect your business and avoid any legal issues. Make sure you research the specific requirements in your location and comply with all necessary regulations, create clear policies and terms of service for your online store, and protect your intellectual property rights to ensure the long-term success of your business.

Chapter 8

Registering Your Business and Obtaining Necessary Permits & Licenses

Starting a dropshipping business requires a few important steps to ensure that your business is legitimate and operating within the confines of the law. One of the most important steps in the process is registering your business and obtaining any necessary permits or licenses.

The first step in registering your business is choosing a business structure. There are several types of business structures to choose from, including sole proprietorship, partnership, LLC, and corporation. Each business structure has its own advantages and disadvantages, so it's important to choose the structure that best fits your specific needs.

Once you've chosen a business structure, the next step is to register your business with the appropriate government agencies. The specific requirements for registering your business will vary depending on your location and the type of business structure you've chosen. Typically, you'll need to register your business with your state government and obtain a tax ID number.

Depending on the nature of your business and your location, you may also need to obtain additional permits and licenses. For example, if you're selling products that are regulated by the FDA or other government agencies, you may need to obtain special permits or licenses. Additionally, some cities and states require specific licenses for certain types of businesses, such as home-based businesses.

Finally, it's important to make sure that you comply with all tax requirements for your business. This may include registering for sales tax, collecting and remitting sales tax on your sales, and paying income tax on your profits. It's important to keep accurate financial records and consult with a tax professional to ensure that you're complying with all tax requirements. Here are some resources to help you navigate the process:

1. SBA.gov - The U.S. Small Business Administration (SBA) is a great resource for entrepreneurs. They offer a step-by-step guide to starting a business, which includes information on registering your business and obtaining permits and licenses.
2. State government websites - Each state has its own requirements for registering a business and obtaining permits and licenses. Visit your state's government website to find out what specific requirements apply to your business.
3. SCORE - SCORE is a nonprofit organization that offers free business advice and mentoring. They have a network of volunteers who can provide guidance on starting and running a business, including registering your business and obtaining permits and licenses.
4. LegalZoom - LegalZoom is an online legal services company that can help you register your business and obtain necessary permits and licenses. They offer a variety of services, including LLC formation, business license research, and more.
5. Business license services - There are a variety of companies that offer business license services. These companies can help you research and obtain the necessary permits and licenses for your business. Some popular options include LicenseLogix and Incfile.

Registering your business and obtaining the necessary permits and licenses is an important step in starting and running a successful dropshipping business. Make sure you choose the appropriate business structure, register your business with the appropriate government agencies, obtain any necessary permits and licenses, and comply with all tax requirements to ensure the long-term success of your business.

Chapter 8

Understanding Taxes & Other Financial Obligations

If you're thinking of starting a dropshipping business, one of the essential things you need to understand is taxes and other financial obligations that come with it. Dropshipping is a popular business model that allows you to sell products without having to hold inventory or manage shipping. However, there are specific financial responsibilities you need to consider ensuring that you're complying with the law and keeping your business financially stable.

One of the critical financial obligations for dropshippers is sales tax. Sales tax is a tax levied on the sale of goods and services. The rules for sales tax vary by state, and it's essential to understand the requirements in your state. As a dropshipper, you need to collect sales tax on the products you sell if you have a sales tax nexus in the state where your customers are located.

A sales tax nexus refers to a connection between a business and a state that triggers a tax obligation. In general, you have a sales tax nexus in a state if you have a physical presence in the state, such as an office, warehouse, or employees. However, other factors can trigger a nexus, such as selling a certain number of products or generating a certain amount of revenue in the state.

To determine your sales tax nexus, you need to review the laws in your state and consult with a tax professional if necessary. Once you've determined your sales tax nexus, you need to register for a sales tax permit with the state and collect sales tax from your customers.

Another financial obligation that you will need to consider is income tax. Income tax is a tax on the income earned by a business or individual. You'll need to pay income tax on the profits earned by your business.

To determine your income tax obligations, you'll need to keep track of your business income and expenses. You can use accounting software to manage your finances and generate reports that show your profit and loss. You'll also need to file an income tax return with the IRS and pay any taxes owed.

As a dropshipper, you're considered self-employed, which means you're responsible for paying self-employment tax. Self-employment tax is a tax on the income earned by self-employed individuals, which includes Social Security and Medicare taxes.

To calculate your self-employment tax, you'll need to use Schedule SE when filing your income tax return. The self-employment tax rate is currently 15.3%, and it applies to the first $142,800 of your net self-employment income.

Aside from taxes, there are other financial obligations that need to be considered. These include:

1. Business licenses and permits: Depending on your state and industry, you may need to obtain business licenses and permits to operate your dropshipping business legally.
2. Shipping and handling costs: You're responsible for shipping and handling costs. These costs can add up, so it's essential to factor them into your pricing strategy.
3. Payment processing fees: When you accept payments from customers, you'll need to pay a processing fee to the payment processor. These fees can vary, so it's important to choose a payment processor that offers competitive rates.
4. Insurance: It's also a good idea to consider insurance to protect your business from liability and other risks.

Starting a dropshipping business can be a profitable venture, but it comes with financial responsibilities. You need to have a firm grasp on your tax obligations, including sales tax, income tax, and self-employment tax, and other financial obligations such as business licenses and permits, shipping and handling costs, payment processing fees, and insurance.

To ensure that you're complying with the law and keeping your business financially stable, it's essential to keep accurate records of your income and expenses and consult with a tax professional if necessary. By understanding and fulfilling your financial obligations, you can set your business up for success and avoid any legal or financial issues down the line.

It's important to note that tax laws and regulations can change, so it's essential to stay up to date on any changes that may affect your business. You can do this by regularly reviewing state and federal tax laws and consulting with a tax professional when necessary.

While taxes and other financial obligations may seem overwhelming, they are a necessary aspect of running a dropshipping business. By understanding and fulfilling these obligations, you can operate your business legally and financially responsibly, setting yourself up for long-term success.

Chapter 8

Creating Policies and Terms of Service for your Online Store

When setting up your dropshipping business, it's important to create policies and terms of service that outline how you will conduct business with your customers. These documents can help you establish expectations and protect yourself legally.

Here are some tips for creating effective policies and terms of service for your online store:

1. Identify your policies: Before you create any policies, you need to identify the areas that you want to cover. Common policies include shipping, returns, refunds, privacy, and security.

2. Be transparent: Your policies and terms of service should be clear and easy to understand. Make sure that your customers can easily find your policies on your website and that they are written in plain language.

3. Be specific: Each policy should be specific and address the most common scenarios. For example, if you have a return policy, it should include information on what items can be returned, how long customers must make a return, and whether or not there are any restocking fees.

4. Protect your business: Your policies and terms of service should also include language that protects your business. For example, you may want to include a clause that limits your liability for damages, or a statement that you have the right to terminate a customer's account for any reason.

5. Consider legal requirements: Depending on where you are located and the products you sell, you may be required to include specific language in your policies and terms of service. For example, if you sell products to customers in the European Union, you will need to comply with the General Data Protection Regulation (GDPR).

6. Update your policies regularly: As your business grows and changes, your policies and terms of service may need to be updated. Make sure to review them periodically and make any necessary changes.

Creating policies and terms of service for your online store is an important step in establishing a professional and trustworthy business. By taking the time to create clear and comprehensive policies, you can build trust with your customers and protect your business from legal issues.

Chapter 8

Protecting Your Intellectual Property Rights and Avoiding Infringement

As a dropshipping business owner, it's important to protect your intellectual property rights and avoid infringing on the rights of others. Intellectual property refers to creations of the mind, such as inventions, literary and artistic works, and symbols, names, and images used in commerce.

Protect Your Intellectual Property Rights & Avoid Infringement

1. Register your trademarks: Trademarks are symbols, names, and phrases that identify and distinguish your brand from others. By registering your trademarks with the appropriate government agency, you can protect your brand and prevent others from using similar marks.

2. Use original content: It's important to use original content on your website and social media accounts to avoid infringing on the copyrights of others. If you use images or written content created by others, make sure you have permission or have purchased the appropriate license.

3. Avoid trademark and copyright infringement: When selecting product names or descriptions, be careful not to use trademarks or copyrighted material belonging to others. Always do your research and make sure you have permission before using any third-party material.

4. Monitor your intellectual property: Keep an eye on the market and monitor for any instances of trademark or copyright infringement. If you find a violation, take swift action to protect your rights.

5. Protect your patents: If you have a unique product or invention, consider filing for a patent to protect your intellectual property. This can be a complex process, so it's best to consult with a patent attorney.

6. Consider using legal tools: There are a variety of legal tools available to protect your intellectual property, such as cease and

desist letters and litigation. If you believe your rights have been violated, consider using these tools to protect your interests.

Here are some resources to help you protect your intellectual property rights and avoid infringement. By utilizing these resources and seeking legal guidance, when necessary, you can protect your intellectual property rights and avoid infringement in your dropshipping business.

1. United States Patent and Trademark Office (USPTO): The USPTO is the federal agency responsible for granting patents and registering trademarks in the United States. Their website provides information on the registration process, as well as resources for enforcing your intellectual property rights. Visit their website at www.uspto.gov.

2. Copyright Office: The Copyright Office is a division of the Library of Congress that registers copyrights for original works of authorship, such as books, music, and art. Their website provides information on copyright registration, as well as resources for resolving copyright disputes. Visit their website at www.copyright.gov.

3. World Intellectual Property Organization (WIPO): WIPO is a specialized agency of the United Nations that promotes and protects intellectual property around the world. Their website provides information on international intellectual property laws, as well as resources for enforcing your intellectual property rights globally. Visit their website at www.wipo.int.

4. LegalZoom: LegalZoom is an online legal services company that offers a variety of tools and resources for protecting your intellectual property rights, such as trademark registration and copyright filings. Visit their website at www.legalzoom.com.

5. Small Business Administration (SBA): The SBA provides resources and guidance for small businesses, including information on intellectual property protection. They also offer training and counseling services to help business owners navigate the legal and regulatory landscape. Visit their website at www.sba.gov.

6. Intellectual Property Owners Association (IPO): The IPO is a trade association that represents owners of patents, trademarks,

copyrights, and trade secrets. Their website provides resources and information on intellectual property laws and policies, as well as networking opportunities with other IP owners. Visit their website at www.ipo.org.

By taking steps to protect your intellectual property rights and avoid infringement, you can build a strong and successful dropshipping business. Don't hesitate to consult with legal professionals to help you navigate the complex world of intellectual property law.

Chapter 9: Creating A Brand for your Dropshipping Business

Chapter 9

The Importance of Branding

In the competitive world of dropshipping, branding is crucial to stand out and build a loyal customer base. A strong brand can differentiate your business, build trust with customers, and drive sales. In this chapter, we'll explore why branding is important and how to develop a strong brand for your dropshipping business.

Branding helps to build trust with customers by providing a consistent and recognizable image of your business. Customers are more likely to do business with a brand that they recognize and trust. A strong brand can create a sense of familiarity and comfort, which can help to drive sales and build customer loyalty.

With so many dropshipping businesses out there, it's important to differentiate yourself from the competition. Branding helps you to create a unique identity and personality for your business, which can set you apart from the competition. By establishing a strong brand, you can create a clear value proposition and communicate your unique selling points to customers.

A strong brand can help to build customer loyalty, which can lead to repeat business and referrals. By creating a positive image and reputation for your business, you can cultivate a loyal following of customers who trust and value your brand.

Branding can also help to drive sales by creating a sense of urgency and desire for your products. By creating a recognizable and appealing brand, you can attract customers who are drawn to your products and message. A strong brand can also help to create a sense of exclusivity and value, which can increase the perceived worth of your products.

Now that we've explored the importance of branding, let's look at how to develop a strong brand for your dropshipping business. To create a strong brand, you need to define your brand identity. This includes your brand values, personality, and voice. Your brand identity should be aligned with your niche and target audience, and it should reflect the unique selling points of your business.

Your visual identity is an important component of your brand. This includes your logo, color palette, typography, and imagery. Your visual identity should be consistent across all marketing channels, including your website, social media, and advertising.

Your brand message should communicate your unique selling points and value proposition. This should be communicated clearly and consistently across all marketing channels. Your brand message should resonate with your target audience and inspire them to act. Here are some resources to help you develop your brand's message:

1. Brand strategy templates - Many organizations publish brand strategy templates to help businesses establish their brand message. These templates typically include questions to help businesses define their brand's values, personality, and unique selling proposition.
2. Competitor analysis tools - Understanding your competitors' brand messages can help you create a message that stands out. Tools like SEMrush and Ahrefs can help you analyze your competitors' marketing strategies and messaging.
3. Customer surveys - Conducting surveys with your target audience can help you understand their needs, preferences, and values. This information can be used to develop a brand message that resonates with your target audience.
4. Social listening tools - Social media listening tools like Hootsuite and Mention can help you monitor social media conversations about your brand and your competitors. This information can be used to identify trends and insights that can inform your brand message.
5. Copywriting courses - Copywriting courses like those offered by Copyblogger and Udemy can help you improve your writing skills and develop a compelling brand message.

6. Brand messaging agencies - Brand messaging agencies like The Creative Company and The Branding Agency specialize in helping businesses develop their brand message. These agencies can provide a range of services including brand messaging workshops, copywriting, and content strategy.

Consistency is key when it comes to branding. Your brand identity, visual identity, and brand message should be consistent across all marketing channels. This helps to create a recognizable and memorable brand that customers can trust and value.

Branding is an essential component of any successful dropshipping business. By building trust with customers, differentiating your business, building customer loyalty, and driving sales, branding can help you to achieve your business goals. By defining your brand identity, creating a visual identity, developing a brand message, and maintaining consistency, you can develop a strong brand that sets your business apart from the competition.

Chapter 9

Developing A Unique Brand Identity and Voice

Developing a unique brand identity and voice is crucial for building a strong and recognizable brand. Before you can create a unique brand identity and voice, you need to define what your brand stands for and the personality you want to convey. Consider what values are important to your brand, what tone of voice you want to use, and what emotions you want to evoke in your audience.

To stand out in a crowded market, you need to understand your target audience and what they're looking for in a brand. Conduct market research to identify what your target audience likes and dislikes, what their pain points are, and what brands they currently engage with.

Your visual brand identity includes your logo, color palette, typography, and any other visual elements that represent your brand. Choose elements that reflect your brand's values and personality and are unique enough to stand out from competitors. Here are some resources to help you develop a brand's visual identity:

1. Canva - Canva is a popular graphic design tool that allows users to easily create stunning designs without any design experience. Canva has a wide range of templates and design elements that can be customized to create a brand's visual identity.
2. Adobe Creative Suite - Adobe Creative Suite is a suite of professional design tools that includes software such as Photoshop, Illustrator, and InDesign. These tools are widely used by professional designers and offer advanced capabilities for creating a brand's visual identity.
3. 99designs - 99designs is a platform that connects businesses with freelance designers who can create custom designs for logos, business cards, websites, and more. The platform offers a variety of design packages at different price points to fit any budget.
4. Branding guidelines templates - Many organizations publish branding guidelines templates to help businesses establish their

brand's visual identity. These guidelines typically include specifications for color, typography, imagery, and graphic elements.

5. Online design communities - There are many online design communities such as Dribbble and Behance where designers showcase their work and connect with other designers. These communities can be a great source of inspiration and can help you find a designer to work with on your brand's visual identity.

Your brand voice should be consistent across all communication channels and reflect your brand's personality. Consider the tone of voice you want to use, the words and phrases that best represent your brand, and any key messaging points you want to convey. Here are some books, websites, and blogs that can service as a wonderful starting point to help you find your brand's voice:

1. Branding Workbook: A Step-by-Step Guide to Creating a Powerful Brand Identity by Fiona Humberstone - This workbook provides exercises and prompts to help you define your brand's personality, values, and voice.

2. The Brand Gap: How to Bridge the Distance Between Business Strategy and Design by Marty Neumeier - This book explains the importance of creating a strong brand identity and how to develop a brand voice that connects with your target audience.

3. StoryBrand by Donald Miller - This book teaches you how to create a clear and compelling brand message that resonates with your audience.

4. Brand Archetypes: 12 Brand Archetypes to Help You Build a Strong Brand by Kathrin Zenkina - This book explores the 12 different brand archetypes and how they can be used to develop a brand identity and voice that resonates with your audience.

5. How to Create a Brand Voice That Connects with Your Target Market by Neil Patel - This article provides practical tips and examples for developing a brand voice that resonates with your target audience.

6. A Guide to Brand Voice by Mailchimp - This resource provides a comprehensive guide to developing a brand voice, including how to define your brand's personality, tone, and language.
7. Branding Strategy Insider - This website provides articles and resources on branding, including how to develop a unique brand identity and voice.
8. Hootsuite Social Media Blog - This blog provides tips and resources for developing a brand voice that resonates on social media, including how to use humor, empathy, and authenticity in your messaging.

Storytelling is a powerful way to connect with your audience and build an emotional connection with your brand. Use stories to illustrate your brand's values, personality, and unique selling proposition.

Consistency is key when it comes to building a strong brand identity and voice. Ensure that your visual and verbal brand elements are consistent across all communication channels and touchpoints.

Once you've developed your brand identity and voice, test it out with your target audience to see how it resonates. Use feedback to refine and improve your brand identity and voice over time.

Developing a unique brand identity and voice takes time and effort, but it's essential for building a strong and recognizable brand. By defining your brand's values and personality, conducting market research, creating a visual brand identity, developing a brand voice, using storytelling, being consistent, and testing and refining, you can create a brand identity and voice that sets you apart from competitors and resonates with your target audience.

Chapter 9

Creating A Memorable Logo and Visual Identity

Your logo and visual identity are essential components of your brand. They represent your business and communicate your brand's message and values. A well-designed logo and visual identity can help you stand out in a crowded marketplace and build brand recognition. Here are some steps to help you create a memorable logo and visual identity:

1. Research your competition: Before you start designing your logo and visual identity, research your competitors to see what kind of logos and visual identities they have. This will help you identify what sets your brand apart and ensure that your logo and visual identity are unique.

2. Define your brand's personality and values: Your brand's personality and values should inform the design of your logo and visual identity. Are you a fun and playful brand, or are you more serious and professional? Are you environmentally conscious, or do you prioritize affordability? Understanding your brand's personality and values will help you create a logo and visual identity that accurately represents your brand.

3. Choose the right colors: Color plays a crucial role in the design of your logo and visual identity. Different colors can evoke different emotions and have different meanings. Choose colors that align with your brand's personality and values and that will resonate with your target audience.

4. Use typography effectively: Typography is another essential element of your visual identity. Choose fonts that are easy to read and that align with your brand's personality and values. Use typography consistently across all your branding materials, including your website, social media, and marketing materials.

5. Keep it simple: A simple, clean logo is often more memorable than a complex one. Avoid using too many colors or intricate designs that may be difficult to reproduce in different formats.

6. Make it versatile: Your logo and visual identity should be versatile enough to use across different mediums and formats. Consider how

your logo will look in different sizes, on different backgrounds, and in black and white.

7. Get feedback: Before finalizing your logo and visual identity, get feedback from others, including friends, family, and your target audience. Use their feedback to refine your design and ensure that your logo and visual identity resonate with your target audience.

8. Work with a professional: Consider hiring a professional graphic designer or branding agency to help you create a unique and memorable logo and visual identity that accurately represents your brand.

When it comes to creating a memorable logo and visual identity, it's important to remember that your brand's personality and values should be at the forefront of your design decisions. You want to create a visual identity that is not only visually appealing but also resonates with your target audience and accurately reflects your brand.

Researching your competition and understanding what sets your brand apart can help you create a unique logo and visual identity. Choosing the right colors and typography, keeping it simple, and making it versatile are all important factors to consider. Additionally, getting feedback from others can help you refine your design and ensure that it resonates with your target audience.

While there are many resources available for creating a memorable logo and visual identity, working with a professional graphic designer or branding agency can provide valuable expertise and ensure that your logo and visual identity accurately represents your brand. Here are some of the more popular resources available to you:

1. Canva: Canva is a graphic design platform that provides templates, tools, and resources to help you create a professional logo and visual identity.

2. 99designs: 99designs is a platform that connects businesses with freelance designers who can help create a logo and visual identity that aligns with your brand's personality and values.

3. Branding Resources by Designhill: Designhill provides a range of branding resources, including logo makers, design templates, and

design contests to help you create a professional logo and visual identity.

4. Fiverr: Fiverr is a freelance platform that offers graphic design services, including logo design and branding packages, at a range of price points.

5. Behance: Behance is a platform where designers can showcase their work, and businesses can find designers to work with on branding projects.

Creating a memorable logo and visual identity is a crucial step in building a strong brand. With the right resources and design decisions, you can create a visual identity that accurately represents your brand and resonates with your target audience.

Chapter 9

Building Brand Recognition and Trust with Customers

Building brand recognition and trust with customers is crucial to the success of any business. It is essential to create a positive image of your brand in the minds of your target audience. Here are some strategies to help you build brand recognition and trust with your customers:

1. Consistency: Consistency is key when it comes to building a recognizable and trustworthy brand. Your brand should have a consistent message, tone, and visual identity across all channels and touchpoints, including your website, social media, email marketing, and customer service interactions.

2. Customer Experience: The customer experience is a critical factor in building trust and loyalty with your customers. Provide excellent customer service, respond quickly to customer inquiries, and go above and beyond to exceed customer expectations. This will help you build a positive reputation and earn the trust of your customers.

3. Social Media Presence: Social media is an excellent tool for building brand recognition and trust with your customers. Consistently post engaging and valuable content on your social media channels, respond to comments and messages promptly, and use social media to build relationships with your audience.

4. Influencer Marketing: Collaborating with influencers in your industry can be an effective way to build brand recognition and trust with your target audience. Partnering with influencers can help you reach new audiences and increase brand credibility and trust.

5. Community Involvement: Getting involved in your local community or supporting a social cause can help build brand recognition and trust with your customers. Consider sponsoring a local event or supporting a charity that aligns with your brand's values.

6. Personalization: Personalization can help you build a deeper connection with your customers and increase brand recognition

and trust. Use data and analytics to personalize your marketing messages and offers and personalize customer experiences whenever possible.

Resources are essential for building brand recognition and trust with customers. Without the right resources, it can be challenging to create a consistent brand message and effectively communicate with your target audience. Resources can help you to streamline your branding efforts and ensure that your message is consistent across all platforms. Additionally, having access to the right resources can help you to build trust with your customers, which is critical for long-term success.

1. HubSpot: HubSpot provides a range of resources, including blog articles, webinars, and templates to help you build brand recognition and trust with your customers.
2. Hootsuite: Hootsuite is a social media management platform that can help you manage your social media presence, engage with your audience, and build brand recognition and trust.
3. Moz: Moz provides SEO tools and resources to help you increase visibility and build brand recognition and trust with your target audience.
4. SurveyMonkey: SurveyMonkey can help you gather feedback from your customers and use that feedback to improve your customer experience and build trust with your audience.

Building brand recognition and trust with customers takes time and effort, but it is crucial for the long-term success of your business. By following the strategies outlined above and utilizing the resources available, you can create a strong, trustworthy brand that resonates with your target audience.

Chapter 9

Tips For Maintaining Brand Consistency Across All Channels

Maintaining brand consistency is essential for building brand recognition and trust with customers. It ensures that your brand is easily identifiable and that customers can quickly recognize your brand's values and personality. Key tips for maintaining brand consistency across all channels:

1. Develop brand guidelines: The first step in maintaining brand consistency is to develop brand guidelines. Brand guidelines outline the visual elements and tone of voice that should be used across all channels, including your website, social media, marketing materials, and customer service communications. This ensures that everyone in your organization understands your brand's identity and can maintain consistency.

2. Use consistent visual elements: Consistent use of visual elements, such as color, typography, and imagery, is critical for maintaining brand consistency. Make sure to use the same color palette and fonts across all channels and use the same style of imagery to create a cohesive look and feel.

3. Maintain a consistent tone of voice: Your brand's tone of voice should be consistent across all channels, from your website and social media to your customer service communications. Whether your brand's voice is playful, professional, or authoritative, make sure it remains consistent to build trust with your customers.

4. Train employees: Make sure all employees, including customer service representatives, understand your brand guidelines and how to communicate with customers in a consistent tone of voice. Consistent messaging from all employees helps to build a cohesive brand identity and increase customer trust.

5. Regularly review and update your brand guidelines: Your brand guidelines should be reviewed regularly to ensure they remain relevant and effective. As your business evolves, your brand identity may change, and your brand guidelines should be updated accordingly.

6. Use technology to maintain consistency: There are several tools and technologies available that can help you maintain brand consistency across all channels. For example, marketing automation tools can help you ensure that all marketing messages are consistent, while digital asset management systems can help you manage your brand's visual assets.

Maintaining brand consistency is crucial for building a strong and recognizable brand identity. By following these tips and utilizing available resources, you can ensure that your brand is consistent across all channels and build trust with your customers. Resources available to you include:

1. Hubspot Branding Guide: Hubspot offers a comprehensive branding guide that covers everything from developing a brand strategy to maintaining brand consistency across all channels.
2. Canva Brand Kit: Canva's Brand Kit is a tool that helps you create and maintain a consistent visual identity for your brand.
3. Brandfolder: Brandfolder is a digital asset management system that helps you manage your brand's visual assets and maintain consistency across all channels.
4. Project Management Tools: Project management tools like Trello and Asana can help you organize your brand assets, such as logos, images, and marketing materials, in one place. This makes it easier to access and share these assets with team members and ensure that they are being used consistently.
5. Social Media Management Tools: Social media management tools like Hootsuite and Sprout Social can help you manage your brand's social media presence and ensure that your messaging and visual identity are consistent across all platforms.
6. Employee Training Programs: Developing employee training programs that focus on brand consistency can help ensure that everyone in your organization understands and upholds your brand's messaging and values. Available training tools include Cornerstone OnDemand, TalentLMS, Adobe Captivate, SAP Litmos, Docebo, Articulate 360, and Moodle.

Maintaining brand consistency across all channels is crucial for building a strong brand and creating a positive brand image. By following the tips discussed in this chapter, such as developing brand guidelines, using consistent visual elements, and regularly monitoring and updating brand messaging, businesses can ensure that their brand is easily recognizable and memorable for their target audience. By consistently delivering a cohesive brand message, businesses can build brand recognition, trust, and loyalty with their customers. Overall, maintaining brand consistency should be a top priority for businesses looking to establish a strong and successful brand.

Charter 10: Analytics & Metrics

Chapter 10

Overview of Key Performance Indicators (KPIs)

In business, Key Performance Indicators (KPIs) are metrics used to evaluate a company's performance and progress towards achieving its objectives. KPIs can help businesses identify areas of strength and weakness, monitor progress towards goals, and make informed decisions. Here are some of the most used KPIs in business:

1. Revenue: Revenue is a key KPI for any business as it directly measures the amount of money generated through sales. It helps businesses evaluate their financial performance and track progress towards their revenue goals.

2. Customer Acquisition Cost (CAC): CAC is the cost of acquiring a new customer. This KPI helps businesses understand the effectiveness of their marketing and sales efforts and helps them make informed decisions about resource allocation.

3. Customer Lifetime Value (CLV): CLV is the total amount of money a customer is expected to spend on a company's products or services over their lifetime. It helps businesses identify their most valuable customers and focus on retaining them.

4. Churn Rate: Churn rate measures the percentage of customers who leave a business over a certain period. It helps businesses understand customer retention and identify areas for improvement in their products or services.

5. Net Promoter Score (NPS): NPS measures customer satisfaction and loyalty by asking customers to rate how likely they are to recommend a business to others. This KPI helps businesses identify areas for improvement in their customer experience and track progress towards increasing customer loyalty.

6. Website Traffic: Website traffic measures the number of visitors to a business's website. It helps businesses understand the effectiveness of their online marketing efforts and identify opportunities to improve website performance.

7. Employee Productivity: Employee productivity measures the efficiency and effectiveness of employees in achieving their goals.

This KPI helps businesses identify areas for improvement in their workforce and make informed decisions about employee training and development.

It's important to note that KPIs may vary depending on the industry, company size, and specific goals of a business. It's essential to identify the most relevant KPIs for your business and regularly track them to evaluate your performance and make informed decisions. Resources for Identifying and Tracking KPIs include:

1. Google Analytics: Google Analytics is a free tool that helps businesses track website traffic and performance metrics.
2. HubSpot: HubSpot provides a range of marketing and sales tools that help businesses track KPIs like CAC and CLV.
3. KPI Library: KPI Library is an online platform that provides a range of KPI templates and resources to help businesses identify and track their KPIs.
4. Microsoft Excel: Microsoft Excel is a powerful tool for creating customized KPI dashboards and tracking KPIs over time.

Key performance indicators (KPIs) are critical for measuring the success of a business or organization. By defining and tracking KPIs, businesses can make data-driven decisions and adjust strategies to achieve their goals. It is important to choose the right KPIs for your business and ensure they are specific, measurable, attainable, relevant, and time bound.

Regular monitoring and analysis of KPIs are necessary for adjusting and improving performance. With the help of KPIs, businesses can stay focused on their objectives and continuously work towards improving their performance and achieving success.

Chapter 10

Understanding Website Analytics and Tracking Tools

In today's digital age, a website is a crucial component of any business's online presence. However, simply having a website is not enough to ensure success. To make informed decisions about your website and improve its performance, you need to understand website analytics and tracking tools. In this chapter, we'll discuss what website analytics are, why they are important, and how to use tracking tools to improve your website's performance.

Website analytics is the collection, measurement, analysis, and reporting of website data. It provides insights into how visitors interact with your website and allows you to track website performance over time. Website analytics can provide valuable information about website traffic, visitor behavior, conversion rates, and much more.

Website analytics provide insights into website performance and allow businesses to make data-driven decisions about their online presence. By tracking website metrics, businesses can identify areas for improvement, understand visitor behavior, and optimize their website for better performance. Website analytics are also essential for measuring the effectiveness of marketing campaigns, improving search engine optimization (SEO), and tracking the return on investment (ROI) of digital marketing efforts.

There are several tracking tools available to businesses to monitor website analytics. Some of the most popular tracking tools include:

1. Google Analytics: Google Analytics is a free web analytics tool that provides businesses with detailed information about website traffic, including visitor behavior, demographics, and acquisition channels.
2. Hotjar: Hotjar is a behavior analytics and user feedback tool that allows businesses to see how visitors interact with their website. It provides heat maps, recordings, and feedback tools to help businesses understand user behavior and optimize their website.

3. SEMrush: SEMrush is an all-in-one digital marketing tool that includes website analytics features. It provides insights into website traffic, backlinks, and competitor data.

4. Crazy Egg: Crazy Egg is a behavior analytics tool that provides businesses with detailed information about visitor behavior, including where visitors click on the website and how far they scroll.

5. Kissmetrics: Kissmetrics is a customer engagement and retention platform that provides businesses with insights into visitor behavior and allows them to track customer journeys and optimize their website for better engagement and conversion rates.

To improve your website's performance using website analytics, follow these steps:

1. Identify your goals: Set clear goals for your website and identify the key performance indicators (KPIs) that will help you track progress towards those goals.

2. Install a tracking tool: Choose a tracking tool that aligns with your goals and install it on your website.

3. Analyze your data: Use the tracking tool to analyze website data and identify areas for improvement. Look for patterns and trends in the data to determine which areas need attention.

4. Take action: Use the insights from website analytics to make data-driven decisions about website design, content, and functionality. Implement changes to optimize website performance and improve the user experience.

Website analytics and tracking tools provide businesses with valuable insights into website performance and allow them to make data-driven decisions about their online presence. By understanding website analytics and using tracking tools, businesses can optimize their website for better performance, improve user experience, and achieve their online goals. Choose the right tracking tool for your business, analyze your data, and take action to improve your website's performance.

Chapter 10

Analyzing Customer Behavior & Identifying Opportunities for Growth

Analyzing customer behavior is a crucial part of growing your business. By understanding how customers interact with your brand and identifying patterns in their behavior, you can identify opportunities for growth and make data-driven decisions to improve your business strategy.

Here are some tips for analyzing customer behavior and identifying opportunities for growth:

1. Use website analytics: Website analytics tools, such as Google Analytics, can provide valuable insights into how customers interact with your website. You can track metrics such as bounce rates, time on page, and conversion rates to identify areas for improvement.
2. Conduct customer surveys: Surveys can help you gather feedback directly from your customers. You can ask questions about their experience with your brand, their purchasing habits, and what they would like to see improved.
3. Monitor social media: Social media platforms offer valuable insights into how customers interact with your brand. You can monitor social media to see what customers are saying about your brand, track engagement rates, and identify opportunities for improvement.
4. Analyze sales data: Sales data can provide insights into which products or services are the most popular and which ones are underperforming. You can use this data to make informed decisions about which products or services to promote and which ones to discontinue.
5. Use customer segmentation: Customer segmentation is the process of dividing customers into different groups based on common characteristics. By segmenting your customers, you can create targeted marketing campaigns and tailor your messaging to specific groups.

6. Monitor customer lifetime value: Customer lifetime value (CLV) is the amount of money a customer is expected to spend on your products or services over their lifetime. By monitoring CLV, you can identify your most valuable customers and create loyalty programs to retain them.

7. Identify areas for improvement: Once you have analyzed customer behavior, use the insights to identify areas for improvement. This could be improving the user experience on your website, creating new products or services to meet customer needs, or offering better customer support.

By analyzing customer behavior and identifying opportunities for growth, you can improve your business strategy and build a loyal customer base. Use a combination of website analytics, customer surveys, social media monitoring, sales data analysis, customer segmentation, CLV monitoring, and identifying areas for improvement to create a comprehensive approach to analyzing customer behavior. Key resources include:

1. Google Analytics: Google Analytics is a free website analytics tool that provides detailed insights into how customers interact with your website.

2. SurveyMonkey: SurveyMonkey is a popular online survey tool that allows you to create and distribute customer surveys.

3. Hootsuite: Hootsuite is a social media management platform that allows you to monitor social media engagement and track customer sentiment.

4. Salesforce: Salesforce is a customer relationship management (CRM) tool that allows you to track customer interactions and analyze sales data. Other CRM companies include Greenrope, Blueshift, and Apptivo.

5. Mixpanel: Mixpanel is an analytics tool that allows you to track user behavior across your website and mobile apps.

By utilizing these resources, you can analyze customer behavior and identify opportunities for growth to take your business to the next level.

Chapter 10

Optimizing Your Website & Marketing Efforts Based on Data

In today's digital age, businesses have access to a wealth of data that can provide insights into customer behavior, website performance, and marketing efforts. By analyzing this data, businesses can make informed decisions and optimize their website and marketing strategies to improve performance and drive growth. Here are some steps to optimize your website and marketing efforts based on data:

1. Set Goals: The first step in optimizing your website and marketing efforts is to set clear, specific goals. This could include increasing website traffic, improving conversion rates, or increasing sales. Having well-defined goals will help you stay focused on what you want to achieve and enable you to track progress and measure success.

2. Analyze Data: To optimize your website and marketing efforts, you need to analyze data to gain insights into customer behavior and identify areas of opportunity. Google Analytics is a popular tool for tracking website metrics such as page views, bounce rates, and conversion rates. Other tools, such as heat mapping software, can provide insights into how customers interact with your website. Analyzing data can help you identify pain points in the customer journey, areas of low engagement, and opportunities for improvement.

3. Test and Experiment: Once you have identified areas for improvement, it's time to test and experiment. A/B testing is a popular method for comparing two versions of a webpage to see which performs better. By testing different website elements, such as headlines, call-to-action buttons, and page layouts, you can make data-driven decisions about what works best for your audience.

4. Personalize the User Experience: Personalization is becoming increasingly important in marketing, and data can help you create a more personalized user experience. By tracking customer behavior and preferences, you can tailor your website and marketing efforts

to meet their needs and provide a more relevant experience. For example, you might send personalized product recommendations based on previous purchases or show different content based on the customer's location or device.

5. Use Data to Inform Marketing Strategy: Data can also help you optimize your marketing efforts. By analyzing data from email campaigns, social media, and other channels, you can identify which channels are most effective and adjust your strategy accordingly. You can also use data to target specific audiences with personalized messaging and optimize your ad campaigns for better ROI.

By optimizing your website and marketing efforts based on data, you can improve customer experience, drive growth, and achieve your business goals. It's essential to regularly review and analyze data to stay ahead of the competition and ensure your website and marketing efforts are always performing at their best. Resources include:

1. Google Analytics: Google Analytics is a free tool that provides website metrics and insights.
2. Crazy Egg: Crazy Egg is a heat mapping tool that provides insights into how customers interact with your website.
3. Optimizely: Optimizely is an A/B testing tool that allows you to test different website elements to improve performance.
4. HubSpot: HubSpot is a marketing automation platform that provides tools for tracking and analyzing marketing data.
5. Mixpanel: Mixpanel is an analytics tool that provides insights into customer behavior and engagement.

It is crucial for businesses to invest in data analytics and continuously monitor their performance to stay ahead of the competition and meet customer needs effectively. Understanding website analytics and tracking tools is essential for making informed decisions about website optimization and marketing efforts. By analyzing customer behavior and identifying opportunities for growth, businesses can optimize their website and marketing strategies based on data-driven insights. This approach can lead to better engagement, increased conversions, and ultimately, improved revenue.

Chapter 10

Using Metrics to Make Informed Business Decisions

In today's business world, data and metrics play an increasingly important role in making informed decisions. Metrics provide a way to measure performance and track progress towards specific goals. With the abundance of data available, it can be overwhelming to determine which metrics to focus on and how to interpret the results. However, understanding and utilizing metrics effectively can lead to improved decision-making, increased efficiency, and better outcomes. Here are some tips for using metrics effectively:

1. Identify the right metrics: Not all metrics are created equal, and not all metrics will be relevant to your business goals. It's important to identify the metrics that will be most useful in helping you make informed decisions. This may include metrics such as revenue, customer acquisition cost, customer lifetime value, conversion rates, and more.

2. Set benchmarks: Once you have identified the metrics that are most relevant to your business, set benchmarks to help you track progress and identify areas for improvement. This can help you set realistic goals and monitor progress towards achieving them.

3. Use data visualization tools: Data visualization tools can help you better understand the data you are analyzing and make it easier to identify patterns and trends. Graphs, charts, and other visual representations can help you quickly and easily identify areas that require attention.

4. Regularly review metrics: It's important to regularly review your metrics and track progress over time. This can help you identify trends and patterns that may not be immediately apparent, as well as areas where you may need to adjust your strategies or tactics.

5. Use metrics to inform decisions: Ultimately, the purpose of tracking metrics is to use the data to make informed business decisions. Use the data you gather to make decisions about where to allocate resources, how to adjust your marketing strategies, and how to improve your overall business operations.

6. Don't rely solely on metrics: While metrics are important, it's important not to rely solely on data when making business decisions. Use your own intuition and experience, as well as feedback from customers and other stakeholders, to make informed decisions.

It's important to identify and invest in the right resources that align with your goals and needs, and to continually evaluate and adjust your approach as your business evolves. Some of the many available metrics-based resources include:

1. Google Analytics: Google Analytics is a free tool that allows you to track website traffic and gather data about your audience.
2. HubSpot: HubSpot is a marketing automation platform that includes tools for tracking metrics such as website traffic, lead generation, and customer acquisition cost.
3. KISSmetrics: KISSmetrics is a web analytics platform that allows you to track metrics related to customer behavior and engagement, such as conversion rates and customer retention.
4. Mixpanel: Mixpanel is a business analytics platform that provides real-time insights into user behavior, allowing you to track metrics related to customer engagement and retention.
5. Tableau: Tableau is a data visualization tool that allows you to create interactive charts, graphs, and other visual representations of your data.

Using metrics to make informed business decisions is critical to the success of any organization. By collecting and analyzing data, businesses can gain valuable insights into their performance and identify areas for improvement. It is essential to choose the right metrics that align with the company's goals and objectives, regularly track and analyze data, and make data-driven decisions. With the right approach to metrics, businesses can optimize their performance, improve customer satisfaction, and ultimately, increase profitability.

Chapter 11: Building Relationships with Suppliers

Chapter 11

Importance Of Building Strong Relationships with Suppliers

A company's suppliers are one of its most critical partners. They provide the necessary raw materials, products, and services that keep the business running. Building strong relationships with suppliers is crucial for the success of any business. It involves establishing positive and mutually beneficial connections with the companies or individuals who supply goods or services to your business. When done effectively, this can help companies to lower their costs, increase efficiency, and enhance the quality of their products or services.

One of the main benefits of building strong relationships with suppliers is cost savings. By cultivating a positive and cooperative relationship, suppliers are often more willing to negotiate prices and provide discounts, which can result in significant cost savings for your business. This can be especially important for small businesses that need to carefully manage their expenses.

Another benefit of strong supplier relationships is increased efficiency. When you have a good relationship with your suppliers, you can work together to streamline processes and eliminate inefficiencies. This can lead to faster turnaround times, improved quality control, and a more responsive supply chain. In turn, this can help you to meet customer demands more effectively and ultimately boost your business's bottom line.

Strong supplier relationships can also lead to better quality products or services. When you work closely with your suppliers, you can communicate your needs and expectations more clearly, allowing them to better understand your business and its unique requirements. This can result in customized products or services that meet your exact specifications, resulting in higher quality and greater customer satisfaction.

Finally, strong supplier relationships can be a valuable source of innovation and competitive advantage. When suppliers are invested in your success, they may be more willing to share new ideas and collaborate on projects that can help your business stay ahead of the competition.

Chapter 11

Establishing Clear Communication & Expectations

Effective communication and clear expectations are essential in any business relationship, especially when it comes to working with suppliers. Establishing a clear line of communication and setting expectations from the outset can help ensure that both parties are on the same page and working towards the same goals. This chapter will discuss the importance of clear communication and expectations, as well as some tips for establishing them in your supplier relationships.

One of the primary benefits of clear communication and expectations is that it helps to build trust and transparency between you and your suppliers. When both parties are clear about what they expect from each other, it helps to prevent misunderstandings and miscommunications that can lead to delays, mistakes, or other issues. This, in turn, can help to strengthen your relationship with your suppliers and lead to more successful business outcomes.

Another benefit of establishing clear communication and expectations is that it can help you to manage your suppliers more effectively. When you have a clear understanding of what your suppliers are responsible for and what they need from you, you can more easily monitor their performance and ensure that they are meeting your standards. This can also help you to identify any issues or areas for improvement early on before they become major problems.

To establish clear communication and expectations with your suppliers, it's important to start by clearly defining your requirements and expectations. This might include things like delivery schedules, quality standards, and payment terms. It's also important to communicate any changes or updates to these requirements as they arise, to ensure that your suppliers are always up to date on your expectations.

Another important aspect of clear communication and expectations is setting up regular check-ins or meetings with your suppliers. This can help you to stay informed about their progress, identify any potential issues early on, and provide feedback or guidance as needed. Regular check-ins can also help to build a stronger relationship with your suppliers and demonstrate that you value their work and contributions to your business.

Clear communication and expectations are crucial for building strong and successful relationships with your suppliers. By setting clear requirements, regularly communicating updates and changes, and establishing regular check-ins or meetings, you can ensure that both parties are on the same page and working towards common goals. This can help to build trust and transparency, improve supplier management, and ultimately lead to more successful business outcomes.

Chapter 11

Negotiating Better Terms and Pricing

Negotiating better terms and pricing is an essential skill for any business owner or procurement professional. It can help you save money, increase profit margins, and build stronger relationships with suppliers. Negotiating requires preparation, effective communication, and a willingness to compromise. In this chapter, we'll discuss tips and strategies for negotiating better terms and pricing with suppliers.

1. Do Your Research: Before entering any negotiation, it's essential to do your research. This includes understanding your own needs and requirements, as well as understanding your supplier's capabilities and limitations. Researching industry standards and benchmarks can also give you leverage in the negotiation and help you understand what is reasonable and achievable. This information can be used to help set realistic goals for the negotiation.

2. Build a Relationship: Building a relationship with your supplier can go a long way in negotiating better terms and pricing. By establishing a good rapport with your supplier, you can create a sense of mutual trust and respect. This can help facilitate more open and honest communication, leading to more productive negotiations. A good relationship can also result in better customer service and faster response times.

3. Focus on Value, Not Just Price: While price is undoubtedly a critical factor in any negotiation, it's important to remember that it's not the only factor. Focusing solely on price can result in a race to the bottom, where quality and service suffer. Instead, focus on the value that your supplier can provide. This includes factors such as delivery times, reliability, and quality. By emphasizing the value of the product or service, you can negotiate better terms and pricing while maintaining a high level of quality.

4. Be Willing to Walk Away: Negotiations can sometimes reach an impasse, where it's not possible to find a mutually acceptable solution. In these cases, it's essential to be willing to walk away.

This demonstrates that you are willing to hold firm on your requirements and that you are serious about finding the best deal possible. Walking away can also give you the leverage to re-approach the supplier later with a better offer.

Negotiating better terms and pricing with suppliers is an essential skill for any business owner or procurement professional. By doing your research, building a relationship, focusing on value, and being willing to walk away, you can negotiate better deals and build stronger relationships with your suppliers. Remember that negotiation is a process, and it may take time to find the best solution for both parties. With persistence and a willingness to compromise, you can achieve better pricing and terms while maintaining a high level of quality and service.

Chapter 11

Collaborating On Marketing and Promotional Efforts

In today's competitive business world, it's important to have strong partnerships with suppliers to create a successful marketing strategy. Collaborating with suppliers on marketing and promotional efforts can help businesses reach a larger audience and increase their customer base. When businesses and suppliers work together, they can pool resources and expertise to create more effective marketing campaigns. Here are some tips for collaborating on marketing and promotional efforts:

1. Identify mutual goals: Before starting a collaboration, it's important to identify common goals. What do both parties hope to achieve from the marketing campaign? Setting clear goals from the outset can help ensure that both parties are working towards the same result.

2. Determine roles and responsibilities: When collaborating on marketing and promotional efforts, it's essential to establish each party's roles and responsibilities. This will help avoid confusion and ensure that each party knows what is expected of them.

3. Share resources and expertise: Collaborating on marketing and promotional efforts allows businesses to pool resources and expertise. Suppliers may have access to marketing data and insights that businesses can use to better target their campaigns. Similarly, businesses may have a deeper understanding of their target audience, which suppliers can use to tailor their messaging.

4. Be flexible and open to new ideas: Collaboration often involves compromise and being open to new ideas. It's important to be flexible and willing to try new approaches to achieve the desired outcome.

5. Communicate regularly: Effective communication is key to any successful collaboration. Regularly scheduled check-ins can help ensure that both parties are on track and can address any issues that arise.

6. Measure and evaluate results: Once the campaign is over, it's essential to measure and evaluate the results. This will help

identify areas of success and areas that need improvement for future campaigns.

Collaborating on marketing and promotional efforts can be a mutually beneficial strategy for businesses and suppliers. By working together, both parties can leverage their strengths and resources to create effective marketing campaigns and reach a larger audience.

Chapter 11

Tips For Maintaining a Positive and Productive Relationship with Suppliers

Maintaining a positive and productive relationship with suppliers is essential for any business that wants to succeed. Strong relationships with suppliers can lead to better pricing, better terms, and access to new products and services. Here are some tips for maintaining a positive and productive relationship with your suppliers:

1. Communicate regularly: Communication is key to any successful relationship, and this is especially true for the relationship between a business and its suppliers. Regular communication helps to ensure that everyone is on the same page and that any issues or concerns can be addressed promptly.

2. Pay on time: Paying your suppliers on time is crucial for maintaining a positive relationship. Late payments can strain the relationship and make it difficult to negotiate better terms and pricing in the future. If you're unable to pay on time, be sure to communicate with your supplier and work out a payment plan.

3. Be transparent: Transparency is essential in any business relationship. Be honest with your suppliers about your needs and expectations and be upfront about any challenges or issues you may be facing. This can help to build trust and strengthen the relationship.

4. Provide feedback: Feedback is important for any supplier to improve their products or services. Be sure to provide constructive feedback to your suppliers so that they can continue to improve and provide better products or services to your business.

5. Collaborate on marketing efforts: Collaborating with your suppliers on marketing efforts can be beneficial for both parties. This can help to increase brand awareness, drive sales, and strengthen the relationship between the two companies.

6. Show appreciation: Finally, showing appreciation for your suppliers is a great way to strengthen the relationship. This can be as simple as sending a thank-you note or providing referrals to other businesses.

Maintaining a positive and productive relationship with your suppliers is essential for the success of your business. By following these tips, you can build strong relationships with your suppliers and enjoy the benefits of better pricing, better terms, and access to new products and services.

Chapter 12:
Dealing with Common Challenges

Chapter 12

Common Challenges

Dropshipping has become a popular business model in recent years, allowing entrepreneurs to start their own e-commerce businesses with relatively low startup costs. However, there are several common challenges that dropshipping business owners may face.

One major challenge is finding reliable suppliers. With dropshipping, the supplier is responsible for fulfilling orders and shipping products directly to the customer, so it is important to find a supplier who is dependable and able to consistently provide high-quality products. Many business owners may need to search through several suppliers before finding one that meets their needs.

Another challenge is managing inventory and stock levels. Because business owners do not physically hold their inventory, it can be difficult to keep track of stock levels and ensure that products are always in stock and available to customers. This can lead to delayed shipping times and lost sales.

Another common challenge is dealing with shipping and delivery issues. Dropshipping business owners may need to rely on their suppliers to handle shipping and delivery, which can lead to issues such as delayed shipments, lost packages, or damaged products. These issues can harm the business's reputation and lead to negative customer reviews.

Lastly, competition can be a major challenge in the industry. With low startup costs and minimal barriers to entry, the market can quickly become saturated with competitors. It is important for business owners to differentiate themselves from their competitors by offering unique products, providing exceptional customer service, and effectively marketing their business.

The dropshipping business can be highly profitable, but it also comes with its own set of challenges. As an entrepreneur in the industry, it is important to be aware of the common challenges that you may encounter and have a plan in place to address them. Some of the key challenges in the business include managing inventory and shipping logistics, competition and pricing pressures, maintaining strong relationships with suppliers, and staying on top of market trends and changes. By staying organized, being proactive, and staying informed, dropshipping entrepreneurs can overcome these challenges and build successful businesses. With the right strategies in place, this business can offer a lucrative opportunity for entrepreneurs who are willing to put in the effort and stay committed to their goals.

Chapter 12

Managing Cash Flow and Staying Profitable

Managing cash flow is one of the most critical aspects of running a successful business, and it's particularly important in the ecommerce world, where margins can be tight and unexpected expenses can crop up at any time. To stay profitable and ensure long-term success, it's important to have a solid grasp on your cash flow situation and take steps to manage it effectively.

The first step in managing your cash flow is to create a budget that accurately reflects your expenses and revenue. This can be a daunting task, particularly for new businesses, but it's essential in order to gain a clear understanding of your financial situation. Be sure to include all of your expenses, from the cost of goods sold to rent, utilities, and marketing expenses, and compare them to your revenue to determine your profit margins. By tracking your expenses and revenue on a regular basis, you'll be able to identify areas where you can cut costs and improve your profitability.

Another key factor in managing cash flow is to keep a close eye on your inventory levels. Overstocking your inventory can tie up valuable cash and prevent you from investing in other areas of your business, while understocking can lead to lost sales and missed opportunities. By tracking your sales and inventory levels closely, you'll be able to determine the optimal inventory levels for your business and avoid overstocking or understocking.

It's also important to stay on top of your accounts receivable and accounts payable. Late payments from customers can cause cash flow problems, while late payments to suppliers can damage your relationships and even result in late fees or interest charges. Consider implementing a system for tracking payments and sending reminders and be sure to follow up promptly on any late payments.

In addition to these tactics, there are several other strategies you can use to manage your cash flow and stay profitable. For example, consider negotiating better terms with your suppliers, such as longer payment terms or bulk discounts. You might also consider offering incentives for early payment from customers, such as a small discount or free shipping.

There are various resources that can help with managing cash flow and staying profitable in a business. Some of these resources include:

1. Accounting software: Accounting software such as QuickBooks, Xero, and FreshBooks can help businesses manage their finances, including cash flow. These tools provide real-time insights into the business's financial health, automate financial processes, and generate reports that help business owners make informed decisions.

2. Financial advisors: Hiring a financial advisor can help businesses make strategic financial decisions, including managing cash flow. Financial advisors can provide expert advice on how to manage cash flow, reduce expenses, and increase profits. They can also help businesses plan and prepare for unforeseen circumstances.

3. Business loans: Business loans can provide businesses with the cash they need to cover short-term expenses and invest in growth. However, it's important to choose the right loan and understand the terms and conditions before taking on debt.

4. Cash flow forecasts: Cash flow forecasts are projections of a business's cash inflows and outflows over a certain period. By forecasting cash flow, businesses can identify potential cash flow gaps and take action to prevent them. This can include adjusting expenses or seeking additional financing.

5. Inventory management software: Inventory management software can help businesses optimize their inventory levels and reduce waste, which can help improve cash flow. By tracking inventory levels and sales data, businesses can identify trends and make data-driven decisions about inventory management.

6. Payment processing tools: Payment processing tools such as PayPal, Stripe, and Square can help businesses streamline their payment processes and get paid faster. By accepting a variety of

payment methods and automating payment processing, businesses can improve cash flow and reduce the risk of late payments.

7. Cash flow management courses: Cash flow management courses can help business owners and managers learn how to manage cash flow effectively. These courses cover topics such as cash flow forecasting, budgeting, and financial analysis, and provide practical tips and strategies for managing cash flow and staying profitable.

Ultimately, the key to managing cash flow and staying profitable is to stay on top of your financial situation and be proactive in addressing any issues that arise. By tracking your expenses and revenue closely, managing your inventory levels, and staying on top of your accounts receivable and accounts payable, you can ensure that your business is operating efficiently and effectively, even in the face of unexpected challenges.

Chapter 12

Dealing With Shipping Delays and Other Logistical Issues

Dealing with shipping delays and other logistical issues can be a major challenge for any business, but it can be especially challenging for e-commerce businesses that rely on timely delivery to keep customers happy. Unfortunately, shipping delays and other logistical issues are a fact of life in the world of e-commerce, and they can be caused by a variety of factors, such as weather events, supply chain disruptions, and human error. However, there are steps that businesses can take to minimize the impact of these issues on their operations.

One key strategy for dealing with shipping delays and logistical issues is to have a backup plan in place. For example, if a shipment is delayed due to a weather event, businesses may be able to reroute the shipment to another location or use a different carrier to ensure that it arrives on time. Additionally, businesses may want to consider maintaining extra inventory on hand to ensure that they can continue to fulfill orders even if there is a delay in the supply chain.

Another important strategy for dealing with shipping delays and logistical issues is to communicate openly and transparently with customers. When a shipment is delayed, businesses should reach out to customers as soon as possible to let them know what is happening and when they can expect their order to arrive. This can help to minimize frustration and maintain customer loyalty.

Businesses may also want to consider investing in shipping and logistics technology to help streamline their operations and reduce the likelihood of delays and other issues. For example, businesses may want to use software to track shipments in real-time, optimize shipping routes, and identify potential supply chain disruptions before they occur.

Finally, businesses should also have a plan in place for how to handle the financial impact of shipping delays and other logistical issues. For example, businesses may need to adjust their pricing or offer refunds to customers if there is a significant delay in their order. By planning and being proactive in their approach to managing shipping delays and other logistical issues, businesses can help to minimize the impact of these challenges on their operations and stay competitive in the world of e-commerce.

Dealing with shipping delays and other logistical issues can be a challenging aspect of running an e-commerce business. Fortunately, there are several resources available to help businesses overcome these obstacles and streamline their shipping processes:

1. Third-Party Logistics Providers (3PLs): 3PLs are specialized logistics companies that offer services such as warehousing, order fulfillment, and shipping. They can help businesses handle their shipping processes more efficiently and effectively, often at a lower cost than handling it in-house. Some popular 3PLs include ShipBob, Red Stag Fulfillment, and ShipMonk.

2. Shipping Software: Shipping software can help businesses manage their shipping processes more effectively by automating tasks such as label printing, order tracking, and delivery notifications. Popular shipping software options include ShipStation, Shippo, and Easyship.

3. Freight Brokers: For businesses that need to ship larger items or quantities, working with a freight broker can help simplify the shipping process. Freight brokers act as intermediaries between businesses and shipping carriers, helping to negotiate better rates and ensure that shipments are delivered on time.

4. Carrier Integration: Many shipping software options offer carrier integration, which allows businesses to easily compare rates and delivery times from multiple carriers. This can help businesses save time and money by selecting the most efficient and cost-effective shipping option for each shipment.

5. Supply Chain Management Software: Supply chain management software can help businesses manage all aspects of their logistics and supply chain, including inventory management, order fulfillment, and shipping. Popular supply chain management software options include TradeGecko, Stitch Labs, and Orderhive.

Chapter 12

Handling Customer Complaints and Negative Reviews

In any business, customer satisfaction is paramount. However, in the dropshipping business, where customers do not have the opportunity to see the product before purchase, the likelihood of negative feedback increases. How a business handles these negative reviews and complaints can make or break its reputation.

1. Respond promptly and professionally: When a customer leaves a negative review or files a complaint, the business owner should respond promptly and professionally. This shows that the business takes customer feedback seriously and is committed to addressing any issues.

2. Acknowledge the customer's experience: Even if the customer's complaint is unfounded, acknowledging their experience can go a long way in resolving the issue. The customer wants to feel heard and understood, and a simple acknowledgment can help achieve this.

3. Offer a solution: Once the business has understood the customer's complaint, it is important to offer a solution. This could include a refund, a replacement product, or any other action that will make the customer feel satisfied.

4. Be transparent: If there is a delay in shipping or a problem with the product, be transparent with the customer. Customers appreciate honesty, and transparency can help build trust.

5. Learn from the feedback: Negative feedback can be a valuable learning opportunity. Use it to identify areas where the business can improve and make changes to prevent similar issues from occurring in the future.

6. Follow up: After the issue has been resolved, it is important to follow up with the customer to ensure their satisfaction. This can help build customer loyalty and prevent negative reviews from being posted online.

7. Encourage positive reviews: To counteract negative reviews, businesses should encourage satisfied customers to leave positive reviews. This can be done through email campaigns or by providing incentives for leaving a review.

By handling negative reviews and complaints in a professional and timely manner, dropshipping businesses can build a positive reputation and establish customer loyalty. Here are some additional tools for your customer service toolkit that will help you prepare to handle must customer service issues:

1. "Hug Your Haters" by Jay Baer: This book provides a comprehensive guide on how to deal with negative customer feedback in the digital age. Baer emphasizes the importance of responding to all feedback, positive or negative, and provides actionable tips for handling different types of complaints.
2. Customer Service Training Courses: These courses teach customer service skills such as active listening, empathy, and conflict resolution. They can help you and your team learn how to handle difficult customers and defuse tense situations.
3. Online Reputation Management Tools: These tools monitor your online presence and alert you to negative reviews or mentions of your business. They can help you stay on top of your online reputation and respond quickly to any negative feedback.
4. Social Media Management Tools: These tools allow you to monitor and manage your social media accounts, including comments and messages. They can help you respond to customer complaints and inquiries in a timely and professional manner.
5. Templates for Responses: Having a set of pre-written responses to common customer complaints or negative reviews can save time and ensure that your responses are consistent and professional. You can find templates and examples online or create your own based on your business's needs.
6. Customer Feedback Surveys: Regularly soliciting feedback from your customers can help you identify areas for improvement and address any issues before they escalate. You can use surveys or

other feedback tools to gather information about your customers' experiences with your business.

7. Training and Support for Employees: Make sure your employees are trained to handle customer complaints and negative reviews, and provide ongoing support and coaching as needed. Encourage them to be empathetic and responsive, and to focus on finding solutions to problems rather than placing blame.

8. Third-Party Mediation Services: In some cases, it may be helpful to bring in a neutral third party to mediate a dispute between you and a customer. This can help defuse tense situations and find a mutually acceptable solution. There are many online mediation services available that specialize in resolving customer disputes.

It is important for dropshipping businesses to prioritize customer satisfaction and to handle negative feedback with care. By acknowledging the customer's experience, offering a solution, and being transparent, businesses can turn a negative experience into a positive one. Additionally, learning from feedback and encouraging positive reviews can help build a strong reputation and drive growth for the business.

Chapter 12

Tips for Staying Resilient and Adapting to Change

In today's fast-paced business world, change is inevitable. Whether it's a shift in market trends, economic downturns, or technological advancements, it's essential to stay resilient and adapt to change to thrive in the long run. Here are some tips for staying resilient and adapting to change in your dropshipping business:

1. Embrace a growth mindset: Adopting a growth mindset means viewing challenges as opportunities for growth and learning. It involves embracing change and being open to new experiences. By developing a growth mindset, you'll be better equipped to handle unexpected changes and challenges in your dropshipping business.
2. Stay informed: Stay up to date on market trends, industry developments, and technological advancements that could impact your dropshipping business. Attend conferences, read industry publications, and network with other entrepreneurs to stay informed and connected.
3. Be proactive: Proactively anticipate potential changes and develop contingency plans to mitigate risks. Consider diversifying your product offerings, exploring new marketing channels, and preparing for economic downturns.
4. Maintain a positive attitude: Maintaining a positive attitude in the face of adversity can help you stay resilient and focused on your goals. Surround yourself with positive influences and seek out support from other entrepreneurs who have faced similar challenges.
5. Embrace innovation: Adopt new technologies, test new marketing strategies, and explore new sales channels to keep your dropshipping business innovative and competitive.

In the ever-evolving world of dropshipping, it is crucial to stay resilient and adaptable to change. With the rise of e-commerce, consumer preferences are constantly shifting, and new challenges arise frequently. It is essential to stay up to date with the latest trends, marketing strategies, and technologies to remain competitive. Fortunately, there are numerous resources available to help entrepreneurs stay resilient and adaptable. Some of the more popular include:

1. Mindset by Carol Dweck: This book explores the power of a growth mindset and how it can lead to success in both personal and professional life.
2. Entrepreneur.com: This website offers a wealth of resources on entrepreneurship, including articles on staying resilient and adapting to change.
3. The Lean Startup by Eric Ries: This book offers a framework for building businesses that can quickly adapt to change and thrive in a fast-paced, unpredictable market.
4. Podcasts: Business and entrepreneurship podcasts such as "How I Built This" and "Entrepreneur on Fire" offer inspiring stories and tips for staying resilient and adapting to change. The EcommerceFuel podcast episodes focus on topics like marketing, logistics, and more. They also feature interviews with successful ecommerce entrepreneurs, who often share their experiences of adapting to changes in the industry.
5. Shopify Blog - The Shopify blog offers a wealth of information on all aspects of ecommerce. They often share tips and strategies for staying resilient in the face of challenges and adapting to changes in the industry.
6. Dropshipping subreddit – The r/dropship and r/dropshipping subreddits are a community of dropshipping entrepreneurs who share tips, strategies, and experiences. It's a great place to connect with other entrepreneurs and learn from their successes and challenges.
7. EcomCrew - EcomCrew is an ecommerce blog and podcast that offers practical advice and strategies for entrepreneurs. They cover topics like product research, marketing, and logistics, and often share tips for staying resilient in the face of challenges.
8. Entrepreneur magazine - Entrepreneur magazine is a great resource for all entrepreneurs, including those in the dropshipping business. They often share stories of successful entrepreneurs who have

faced challenges and adapted to change and offer practical tips for staying resilient in the face of adversity.

9. LinkedIn Learning - LinkedIn Learning offers courses on a variety of business topics, including ecommerce and dropshipping. They have courses focused on building resilience, managing change, and developing a growth mindset, which can be valuable for emerging entrepreneurs.

Adapting to change and staying resilient is crucial for any dropshipping business to succeed in the long term. The resources mentioned in this chapter provide a wealth of knowledge and practical tips for staying resilient during tough times, adapting to change, and maintaining a growth mindset. Whether it's overcoming shipping delays, managing cash flow, or dealing with customer complaints, the right mindset and resources can make all the difference.

Chapter 13: Success Stories & Case Studies

Chapter 13

Real-Life Success Stories

The dropshipping business model has gained immense popularity in recent years, and many entrepreneurs have leveraged it to build successful businesses. In this chapter, we will explore some real-life success stories and the strategies they used to achieve success.

Gymshark

Gymshark is a fitness apparel and accessories company that was founded in 2012 by Ben Francis. The company started as a dropshipping business, with Francis designing and selling fitness apparel from his bedroom. Gymshark quickly gained popularity through social media marketing and the company's focus on innovation and high-quality products. In 2020, Gymshark was valued at over $1.3 billion and has been named the fastest-growing company in the UK. While the company has now moved away from the dropshipping model, it credits its early success to the model's ability to allow the company to scale quickly and efficiently. The company's success can be attributed to its focus on social media marketing, which helped it gain a loyal following of fitness enthusiasts. Gymshark collaborated with social media influencers to showcase its products, and this helped it reach a wider audience. The company also leveraged user-generated content and engaged with its followers on social media to build a strong community.

Hubble Contacts

Hubble Contacts is a New York-based company that specializes in affordable daily contact lenses. The company was founded in 2016 by Jesse Horwitz and Ben Cogan. Hubble Contacts utilizes the dropshipping business model to keep costs low and to be able to offer affordable prices to its customers. The company has been successful in attracting a large customer base through its subscription-based model and its competitive pricing. As of 2021, the company has raised over $73 million in funding and has been valued at over $200 million.

Beardbrand

Beardbrand is a men's grooming company that was founded in 2012 by Eric Bandholz. The company specializes in high-quality grooming products for beards and has a loyal customer base. Beardbrand utilizes the dropshipping model to fulfill its orders, allowing the company to focus on product development and marketing. The company has been successful in building a strong brand and has been featured in numerous media outlets. As of 2021, the company has over 500,000 followers on social media and has expanded its product line to include hair and body products.

Mokosh

Mokosh is an Australian skincare brand that was founded by Marion O'Leary in 2012. The company uses only organic and fair-trade ingredients and follows a sustainable and ethical business model. Mokosh started as a small business selling handmade skincare products at local markets. O'Leary later expanded her business by partnering with a dropshipping supplier, which allowed her to reach a wider audience. The company's success can be attributed to its focus on quality and sustainability, which resonated with its customers. Mokosh also leveraged social media marketing and engaged with its customers to build a loyal following.

SkinnyMe Tea

SkinnyMe Tea is an Australian-based company that sells detox teas and weight-loss programs. The company was founded by Gretta van Riel in 2012 and grew rapidly, with over $600,000 in revenue in its first year. SkinnyMe Tea started as a dropshipping business, with van Riel outsourcing the manufacturing and shipping to suppliers. The company's success can be attributed to its focus on influencer marketing, which helped it gain a large following on social media. SkinnyMe Tea collaborated with social media influencers to promote its products, and this helped it reach a wider audience. The company also leveraged user-generated content and engaged with its customers on social media to build a strong community.

These real-life success stories demonstrate that the dropshipping business model can be a viable option for entrepreneurs looking to build successful businesses. By focusing on quality products, social media marketing, and building a loyal community, these businesses were able to achieve rapid growth and success.

Chapter 13

Case Studies: Overcoming Challenges & Achieving Growth

Dropshipping can be a challenging business, with numerous hurdles to overcome. However, many businesses have been able to overcome these challenges and achieve growth. In this chapter, we will look at some case studies of businesses that have successfully navigated the challenges of dropshipping and achieved significant growth.

Gymshark

Gymshark is a fitness apparel company that was founded in 2012. The company started as a dropshipping business and has since grown into a multimillion-dollar enterprise. In the early days, Gymshark faced a number of challenges, including issues with shipping and delivery times. To overcome these challenges, Gymshark invested in their own warehousing and logistics systems. By taking control of their own supply chain, they were able to improve their delivery times and provide a better customer experience. In addition, Gymshark invested heavily in influencer marketing, which helped them build a strong brand and gain a loyal following.

Wayfair

Wayfair is an e-commerce company that specializes in home goods and furniture. The company was founded in 2002 and started out as a dropshipping business. However, as the company grew, they faced quite a few challenges, including difficulties in managing inventory and maintaining profitability. To overcome these challenges, Wayfair invested heavily in their technology infrastructure, including developing their own proprietary software to manage inventory and logistics. In addition, the company made a concerted effort to build strong relationships with suppliers, negotiating better terms and pricing to help improve their margins.

ColourPop Cosmetics

ColourPop Cosmetics is a makeup brand that was founded in 2014. The company started as a dropshipping business and has since grown into a major player in the beauty industry. ColourPop faced several challenges in the early days, including issues with product quality and supply chain management. To overcome these challenges, the company invested heavily in their own manufacturing facilities, which allowed them to maintain greater control over the production process and improve product quality. In addition, ColourPop embraced social media marketing, building a strong following on platforms like Instagram and leveraging influencer partnerships to drive sales.

Beardbrand

Beardbrand is a men's grooming company that was founded in 2012. The company started as a dropshipping business and has since grown into a successful e-commerce enterprise. Beardbrand faced numerous challenges in the early days, including difficulties in sourcing quality products and building a strong brand identity. To overcome these challenges, Beardbrand focused on building a strong community around their brand, leveraging social media to engage with customers and build a loyal following. In addition, the company invested heavily in content marketing, producing high-quality videos and blog posts that helped establish Beardbrand as an authority in the men's grooming space.

These case studies demonstrate that success in dropshipping requires a combination of innovative thinking, strategic investments, and a willingness to adapt and overcome challenges. By investing in their own infrastructure, building strong relationships with suppliers, and embracing social media and influencer marketing, these companies were able to achieve significant growth and success in the highly competitive world of dropshipping.

Chapter 13

Lessons Learned

The world of dropshipping is constantly evolving and can be challenging for even the most seasoned entrepreneurs. However, by learning from the experiences of successful dropshippers who have navigated the ups and downs of the industry, aspiring entrepreneurs can avoid common mistakes and build successful businesses. Here are some lessons learned from successful dropshipping entrepreneurs:

1. Focus on providing value to customers: Many successful dropshippers emphasize the importance of providing high-quality products and exceptional customer service. By focusing on delivering value to customers, businesses can build loyal customer bases and increase their chances of long-term success.
2. Embrace automation and technology: Successful dropshippers understand the importance of leveraging technology to streamline processes and automate repetitive tasks. By embracing automation, businesses can reduce costs and increase efficiency, freeing up time and resources to focus on growing the business.
3. Build a strong brand: Building a strong brand is critical to the success of any dropshipping business. By creating a strong brand identity, businesses can differentiate themselves from competitors and establish themselves as trusted and reliable sources of high-quality products.
4. Constantly adapt and evolve: The dropshipping industry is constantly changing, and successful dropshippers understand the importance of being adaptable and evolving with the times. By staying on top of trends and adapting to new market conditions, businesses can stay ahead of the competition and continue to grow and thrive.
5. Focus on marketing and customer acquisition: Marketing and customer acquisition are key drivers of success in the dropshipping industry. Successful dropshippers understand the importance of investing in effective marketing strategies to attract new customers and build brand awareness.

By learning from the experiences of successful dropshippers, aspiring entrepreneurs can gain valuable insights into what it takes to build a successful dropshipping business. By focusing on providing value to customers, embracing technology, building a strong brand, constantly adapting and evolving, and investing in effective marketing strategies, dropshippers can increase their chances of long-term success in this dynamic and challenging industry.

Chapter 13

Our Purpose is to Inspire

Starting your own dropshipping business can be a daunting task, but it can also be incredibly rewarding. It requires a lot of hard work, dedication, and determination to succeed, but the potential for financial freedom and personal fulfillment is worth the effort. In this chapter, we will explore some inspiring stories of successful dropshipping entrepreneurs and provide you with tips and motivation to help you pursue your own dropshipping venture.

One of the most inspiring stories of dropshipping success is that of Richard Lazazzera, the founder of A Better Lemonade Stand. After working in the e-commerce industry for several years, Richard decided to start his own online store. He faced several challenges along the way, including finding the right product and supplier, developing a brand, and creating an effective marketing strategy. However, he persevered and grew his store into a successful business that offers valuable resources for other aspiring entrepreneurs.

Another inspiring story is that of Michael Ugino and Jon Wheatley, the founders of Brickell Men's Products. They started their business in 2014 with a small line of men's grooming products and have since grown it into a multimillion-dollar brand. They attribute their success to a commitment to quality and a dedication to providing exceptional customer service.

These success stories demonstrate that anyone can succeed in the dropshipping business with hard work, dedication, and a willingness to learn and adapt. They also provide valuable lessons that can help you avoid common pitfalls and achieve your own success.

If you're feeling overwhelmed or unsure about starting your own dropshipping venture, there are many resources available to help you. Online forums and communities, such as the Shopify Community and Reddit's r/dropship, offer a wealth of knowledge and support from fellow entrepreneurs. E-commerce platforms like Shopify and BigCommerce offer user-friendly tools and resources to help you get started, including customizable website templates, payment processing, and marketing integrations.

It's also important to remember that success in dropshipping is not guaranteed overnight. It takes time, effort, and patience to build a successful business. But with the right mindset and approach, it's possible to achieve your goals and turn your dreams into reality.

Starting a business can be a challenging yet rewarding venture. There are many successful entrepreneurs who have paved the way and offer valuable lessons and inspiration. By staying motivated, learning from others, and utilizing available resources, you can build a successful and fulfilling dropshipping business.

"Success is not final, failure is not fatal: it is the courage to continue that counts." - Winston Churchill

Chapter 14: Conclusion

Chapter 14

Key Takeaways

Throughout this guide, we have covered a wide range of topics related to the dropshipping business. From understanding the basics of dropshipping to marketing strategies, inventory management, and future trends, we have provided insights and practical tips to help you succeed in this industry. Now, let's take a step back and summarize the key takeaways from all the previous questions. These takeaways will serve as a comprehensive guide for anyone looking to start or grow their business:

1. Dropshipping is a low-risk and cost-effective way to start an ecommerce business. It allows entrepreneurs to focus on marketing and customer acquisition rather than inventory management.

2. Choosing the right niche is crucial for success. Conducting market research, identifying customer needs and preferences, and staying current with industry trends can help in identifying profitable niches.

3. Partnering with reliable and efficient suppliers is essential for smooth operations. Building strong relationships with suppliers can lead to better pricing, faster shipping times, and higher product quality.

4. Optimizing product pages, advertising campaigns, and logistics processes can improve profitability and increase customer satisfaction. Regularly reviewing and analyzing data can help identify areas for improvement.

5. Marketing and advertising are essential for success. Utilizing multiple channels such as paid advertising, social media, and email marketing can help drive traffic to your store and increase sales.

6. Managing your inventory and orders is crucial for a smooth and successful operation. Using tools for automatic order processing, streamlining your logistics and fulfillment process, and offering efficient returns and customer service can all help improve your business.

7. Outsourcing tasks can free up time for entrepreneurs to focus on core business activities and growth strategies.

8. Keeping an eye on future trends and predictions in the industry can help entrepreneurs stay ahead of the competition and adapt to changing market conditions.

Overall, running a successful dropshipping business requires careful planning, ongoing optimization, and a willingness to adapt to changing market conditions. By following these key takeaways, entrepreneurs can maximize their chances of success in the competitive world of ecommerce.

Chapter 14

Final Thoughts

As we come to the end of this book, I want to leave you with some final thoughts. Starting a dropshipping business can seem overwhelming, but I hope this guide has shown you that with the right strategies and mindset, anyone can succeed in this industry.

Remember, success doesn't come overnight, but with patience, perseverance, and a willingness to learn and adapt, you can build a thriving business. Don't be afraid to take risks, try new things, and continuously improve your processes.

Most importantly, always prioritize your customers and their needs. Provide exceptional customer service and strive to offer high-quality products that bring value to their lives. If you keep your customers at the center of your business, everything else will fall into place.

Lastly, never forget that entrepreneurship is a journey, and the most important thing is to enjoy the ride. Embrace the challenges and celebrate your successes, big or small. I hope this book has given you the knowledge and confidence to embark on this journey. Good luck and happy dropshipping!

"The only limit to our realization of tomorrow will be our doubts of today." - Franklin D. Roosevelt

Chapter 15: Bonus Content For 2023

Chapter 15

Top 20 Niches Featuring 189 Top Products

Here are some of the top categories and their respective top selling items that I have been compiling in 2023. I hope you find them as useful as I have.

Fitness Equipment & Accessories

1. Resistance bands - Resistance bands are versatile and can be used for a variety of workouts, making them popular among fitness enthusiasts.
2. Yoga mats - Yoga mats are an essential item for anyone practicing yoga, and they come in a variety of styles and colors.
3. Foam rollers - Foam rollers are used for self-myofascial release, which helps with muscle recovery and pain relief.
4. Workout gloves - Workout gloves protect the hands during weightlifting and other exercises, and they come in a variety of styles and materials.
5. Weighted vests - Weighted vests are popular among fitness enthusiasts who want to add extra resistance to their workouts.
6. Dumbbells - Dumbbells are a classic piece of fitness equipment that are used for a variety of exercises, from bicep curls to shoulder presses.
7. Jump ropes - Jump ropes are a simple and effective tool for cardio workouts, and they come in a variety of styles and materials.
8. Kettlebells - Kettlebells are a versatile piece of equipment that can be used for strength and cardio workouts.
9. Exercise balls - Exercise balls are popular for core workouts and balance training, and they come in a variety of sizes and materials.
10. Running shoes - Running shoes are an essential item for anyone who enjoys running or jogging, and there are many different styles and brands available to choose from.

Beauty & Skincare Products

1. Facial cleansers - Facial cleansers are an essential part of any skincare routine and are used to remove dirt, oil, and makeup from the face.

2. Moisturizers - Moisturizers are used to hydrate the skin and prevent dryness and are available in a variety of formulations for different skin types.

3. Face masks - Face masks are popular for deep cleansing, exfoliation, and brightening the skin, and they come in a variety of types, such as sheet masks, clay masks, and peel-off masks.

4. Serums - Serums are highly concentrated formulations that are used to target specific skincare concerns, such as fine lines, dark spots, and acne.

5. Sunscreen - Sunscreen is essential for protecting the skin from sun damage and is available in a variety of formulations, including lotions, sprays, and creams.

6. Lip balms - Lip balms are used to hydrate and protect the lips from dryness and cracking, and they come in a variety of flavors and formulations.

7. Eye creams - Eye creams are formulated specifically for the delicate skin around the eyes and are used to target concerns such as dark circles, puffiness, and fine lines.

8. Hair care products - Hair care products, such as shampoos, conditioners, and styling products, are essential for maintaining healthy and beautiful hair.

9. Nail care products - Nail care products, such as nail polishes, removers, and treatments, are essential for maintaining healthy and beautiful nails.

10. Makeup - Makeup products, such as foundations, powders, and lipsticks, are popular for enhancing beauty and creating different looks.

Pet Products & Accessories

1. Dog beds - Dog beds are essential for providing comfort and support to pets and come in a variety of styles and sizes.

2. Dog food and treats - Dog food and treats are essential for maintaining the health and well-being of pets and are available in a variety of formulations and flavors.

3. Dog toys - Dog toys are popular for keeping pets entertained and stimulating their minds, and they come in a variety of styles and materials.

4. Dog collars and leashes - Dog collars and leashes are essential for keeping pets safe and under control while out in public, and they come in a variety of styles and materials.

5. Cat litter and litter boxes - Cat litter and litter boxes are essential for maintaining the cleanliness and hygiene of the home and come in a variety of formulations and styles.

6. Cat toys - Cat toys are popular for keeping pets entertained and stimulating their minds, and they come in a variety of styles and materials.

7. Bird cages and accessories - Bird cages and accessories are essential for providing a comfortable and safe environment for pet birds and come in a variety of sizes and styles.

8. Fish tanks and aquarium accessories - Fish tanks and aquarium accessories are essential for providing a comfortable and safe environment for pet fish and come in a variety of sizes and styles.

9. Small animal cages and accessories - Small animal cages and accessories, such as hamster wheels and tunnels, are essential for providing a comfortable and stimulating environment for small pets.

10. Pet grooming products - Pet grooming products, such as brushes, combs, and shampoos, are essential for maintaining the health and appearance of pets and come in a variety of formulations and styles.

Baby Products & Accessories

1. Baby strollers - Baby strollers are essential for transporting infants and toddlers and come in a variety of styles and configurations.
2. Diapers - Diapers are essential for maintaining the hygiene and comfort of babies and come in a variety of styles and sizes.
3. Baby bottles and feeding accessories - Baby bottles and feeding accessories, such as nipples and bottle brushes, are essential for feeding infants and come in a variety of styles and materials.
4. Baby carriers and wraps - Baby carriers and wraps are popular for keeping infants close and comfortable while allowing parents to be hands-free, and they come in a variety of styles and materials.
5. Baby monitors - Baby monitors are essential for keeping an eye and ear on infants and come in a variety of styles and configurations.
6. Baby cribs and bassinets - Baby cribs and bassinets are essential for providing a safe and comfortable sleeping environment for infants and come in a variety of styles and materials.
7. Baby clothing and accessories - Baby clothing and accessories, such as onesies, bibs, and hats, are essential for keeping infants comfortable and stylish.
8. Baby car seats - Baby car seats are essential for providing safety and protection while transporting infants and toddlers in vehicles and come in a variety of styles and configurations.
9. Baby bath products - Baby bath products, such as shampoos, soaps, and lotions, are essential for maintaining the hygiene and health of infants and come in a variety of formulations and styles.
10. Baby teething toys and pacifiers - Teething toys and pacifiers are essential for soothing infants and helping with the teething process, and they come in a variety of styles and materials.

Fashion & Apparel

1. T-Shirts: A wardrobe staple, T-shirts are comfortable and versatile, and come in a wide variety of styles and designs.

2. Jeans: Another wardrobe essential, jeans are durable, comfortable, and come in many styles and cuts to fit various body types and fashion preferences.

3. Sneakers: Sneakers are a popular footwear choice for their comfort and versatility. They can be worn with a variety of outfits, from casual to athletic.

4. Dresses: Dresses come in a variety of styles, lengths, and designs, and can be dressed up or down depending on the occasion. They are a popular choice for special events or formal occasions.

5. Leggings: Comfortable and versatile, leggings have become a popular fashion trend in recent years and can be worn with a variety of tops and shoes.

6. Hoodies: Hoodies are a comfortable and casual clothing item, often worn for lounging or during athletic activities.

7. Sunglasses: Sunglasses not only protect your eyes from the sun's harmful rays, but also add a stylish touch to any outfit.

8. Backpacks: Backpacks are a practical accessory for carrying daily essentials and come in a variety of styles and designs to fit any fashion preference.

9. Watches: Watches are not only functional for telling time, but also add a stylish touch to any outfit. They come in a variety of styles, from casual to formal.

10. Scarves: Scarves are a versatile accessory that can be worn in a variety of ways and can add a pop of color or pattern to any outfit.

Home Decor & Furniture Category

1. Area rugs - These can add color and warmth to any room and come in a variety of materials, sizes, and patterns.
2. Wall art and decor - Including framed prints, canvas art, and metal wall decor. These items can add personality and style to any space.
3. Throw pillows - These can be easily swapped out to update the look of a room and come in a range of colors, patterns, and textures.
4. Sofas and sectionals - A staple in most living rooms, these come in various sizes, materials, and colors to fit any style and budget.
5. Dining tables and chairs - These are essential pieces of furniture for any dining room or eat-in kitchen and come in a variety of styles and finishes.
6. Bedding and linens - Including sheets, comforters, duvets, and pillowcases. These items can help create a cozy and comfortable bedroom.
7. Lighting - Table lamps, floor lamps, and overhead fixtures can add both function and style to a room.
8. Storage solutions - Such as bookcases, shelves, and cabinets, can help keep a space organized while also adding visual interest.
9. Accent chairs - These can add extra seating and a pop of color or texture to a room.
10. Decorative objects - Including vases, sculptures, and figurines, can add interest and style to shelves, tables, and other surfaces.

Electronics & Gadgets

1. Smartphones: iPhones, Samsung Galaxy, and other high-end smartphones are always in demand.
2. Laptops and tablets: With the increase in remote work and virtual learning, laptops and tablets have become essential for many people.
3. Smart home devices: Smart speakers, thermostats, security cameras, and other devices that can be controlled via voice or smartphone are increasingly popular.
4. Gaming consoles: Consoles like PlayStation, Xbox, and Nintendo Switch continue to be top sellers.
5. Headphones: Wireless headphones and earbuds are a popular choice for many consumers, especially those who enjoy music and podcasts.
6. Wearable technology: Fitness trackers and smartwatches that can monitor health and activity levels are popular.
7. Drones: Consumer drones have become increasingly popular for photography and videography enthusiasts.
8. Smart TVs: Televisions with built-in streaming capabilities and voice control are growing in popularity.
9. Cameras: High-end DSLR cameras and mirrorless cameras are popular with photography enthusiasts.
10. Virtual reality devices: Virtual reality headsets and accessories are becoming more accessible and affordable, making them a growing market.

Toys & Games

1. Board games and puzzles - These timeless classics have seen a resurgence in popularity, with many people turning to them as a source of entertainment and family bonding during the pandemic.

2. Action figures and collectibles - Fans of franchises such as Star Wars, Marvel, and DC Comics are always on the lookout for the latest action figures and collectibles to add to their collections.

3. STEM toys - With an increased emphasis on science, technology, engineering, and mathematics education, STEM toys have become increasingly popular for children of all ages.

4. Outdoor and sports toys - With the rise of outdoor activities and sports, toys that promote physical activity and outdoor play, such as bikes, scooters, and sports equipment, are always in demand.

5. Dolls and accessories - Dolls have been a popular toy for generations, and with new accessories and playsets constantly being released, this category continues to be a top seller.

6. Arts and crafts - With many children spending more time at home, arts and crafts have become a popular pastime and a way to foster creativity and imagination.

7. Educational toys - Educational toys that promote learning and development, such as building blocks, alphabet and number games, and musical instruments, continue to be popular with parents and caregivers.

8. Remote control toys - Remote control cars, helicopters, and drones remain popular with both children and adults, providing hours of entertainment and excitement.

9. Plush toys - Stuffed animals and plush toys are a staple in the toy industry, with new characters and designs constantly being introduced.

10. Interactive toys - Interactive toys that respond to touch or voice commands, such as robotic pets and smart toys, have become increasingly popular in recent years.

Outdoor & Camping Gear

1. Tents - Tents are a staple item for anyone who loves the great outdoors. From small, lightweight backpacking tents to large family-sized tents, there are many different styles and designs to choose from.

2. Sleeping bags - A good quality sleeping bag is essential for staying warm and comfortable during camping trips. There are many different types of sleeping bags available, from lightweight summer bags to heavy-duty winter bags.

3. Backpacks - A durable and comfortable backpack is an essential item for anyone who enjoys hiking or camping. There are many different types of backpacks available, from small daypacks to large multi-day backpacks.

4. Camping chairs - Camping chairs are a popular item for those who enjoy spending time outdoors. There are many different types of chairs available, from lightweight portable chairs to heavy-duty, reclining chairs with built-in cup holders.

5. Portable grills - A portable grill is a great item for anyone who enjoys cooking and eating outdoors. There are many different types of grills available, from small charcoal grills to large propane grills with multiple burners.

6. Water bottles - Staying hydrated is essential when spending time outdoors, and a good quality water bottle is a must-have item. There are many different types of water bottles available, from lightweight plastic bottles to heavy-duty stainless-steel bottles.

7. Hiking boots - A good pair of hiking boots is essential for anyone who enjoys hiking or backpacking. There are many different types of boots available, from lightweight trail runners to heavy-duty mountaineering boots.

8. Headlamps - A reliable headlamp is an essential item for anyone who spends time outdoors after dark. There are many different types of headlamps available, from small, lightweight models to heavy-duty, waterproof models with multiple brightness settings.

9. Portable power banks - Portable power banks are a popular item for those who like to stay connected while spending time outdoors. There are many different types of power banks available, from

small, pocket-sized models to large, high-capacity models that can charge multiple devices at once.

10. Hammocks - Hammocks are a popular item for those who enjoy relaxing outdoors. There are many different types of hammocks available, from lightweight, portable models to large, sturdy hammocks that can support multiple people at once.

Health & Wellness Products

1. Supplements and vitamins: Dietary supplements, vitamins, and minerals are always in high demand among health-conscious consumers.

2. Fitness trackers: Wearable devices such as Fitbit and Apple Watch have become increasingly popular for tracking physical activity, sleep patterns, and other health metrics.

3. Essential oils and aromatherapy diffusers: Essential oils and diffusers are commonly used for relaxation, stress relief, and other wellness purposes.

4. Yoga mats and accessories: Yoga has gained widespread popularity in recent years, making yoga mats, blocks, and other accessories a popular item for fitness enthusiasts.

5. Massagers: Electric massagers and massage guns are popular items for people seeking relief from sore muscles and tension.

6. Air purifiers and humidifiers: Air purifiers and humidifiers can improve air quality and reduce allergens, making them popular for people with respiratory issues or allergies.

7. Personal care products: Items such as skincare products, natural and organic beauty products, and personal care items like electric toothbrushes and water flossers are also popular in the health and wellness category.

Jewelry and Accessories

1. Necklaces - Necklaces are a popular jewelry item that can range from simple and delicate to bold and statement-making. They can be made from various materials such as gold, silver, and beaded designs.
2. Earrings - Earrings come in various styles, including studs, hoops, and dangle earrings. They are a popular accessory that can add a touch of elegance or boldness to any outfit.
3. Bracelets - Bracelets are a popular accessory that can be worn alone or layered for a more dramatic effect. They come in different styles, including bangles, cuffs, and beaded designs.
4. Watches - Watches are a functional and fashionable accessory that can be worn by both men and women. They come in various styles and designs, from classic leather straps to modern smartwatches.
5. Sunglasses - Sunglasses are a staple accessory for protecting your eyes from the sun's harmful rays. They come in various shapes and styles, from classic aviators to trendy oversized frames.
6. Handbags - Handbags are not only functional for carrying your belongings but also a fashion statement. They come in various styles, including totes, clutches, and crossbody bags.
7. Rings - Rings are a popular jewelry item that can be worn as a statement piece or stacked for a more personalized look. They come in various styles, including stackable rings, cocktail rings, and engagement rings.
8. Scarves - Scarves are a versatile accessory that can be worn in various ways, such as around the neck or as a headband. They come in different materials such as silk, wool, and cotton.
9. Hair Accessories - Hair accessories, such as hair clips and headbands, have become a popular trend in recent years. They can add a touch of glam or simplicity to any hairstyle.
10. Brooches - Brooches are a timeless accessory that can be worn on clothing, hats, or bags. They come in various designs, including vintage and modern styles.

Craft Supplies & DIY Kits Category

1. Sewing kits: With the rise of the slow fashion movement, many people are looking to learn how to sew or mend their clothes, leading to an increase in sales of sewing kits.

2. Art supplies: From watercolor paints to calligraphy pens, art supplies are always in demand for both professionals and hobbyists alike.

3. Knitting and Crochet kits: Knitting and crochet have become increasingly popular in recent years, and many people are looking for beginner-friendly kits to get started.

4. DIY home decor kits: Customers love to create unique and personalized decor items for their homes, such as macrame wall hangings, terrariums, and candle-making kits.

5. Scrapbooking supplies: Scrapbooking has been a favorite pastime for many years, and it shows no signs of slowing down, with many people looking for unique supplies to make their scrapbooks stand out.

6. Jewelry-making kits: From beading to wire wrapping, customers love the ability to create their own unique jewelry pieces with easy-to-use kits.

7. Soap-making kits: The popularity of natural and handmade soaps has led to an increase in demand for soap-making kits that allow customers to create their own custom soaps.

8. DIY leatherworking kits: Leatherworking is a popular hobby, and many customers are looking for beginner-friendly kits to get started, such as making their own wallets or belts.

9. Candle-making kits: Candles are a popular home decor item, and customers love the ability to create their own custom scents and designs with easy-to-use kits.

10. DIY woodworking kits: Woodworking has become increasingly popular in recent years, and many customers are looking for beginner-friendly kits to get started, such as making their own cutting boards or picture frames.

Kitchen & Dining Products

1. Kitchen gadgets and tools such as vegetable slicers, graters, and garlic presses
2. Cookware sets and individual pots and pans, especially those with non-stick coatings.
3. Cutlery sets and individual knives, including chef's knives, bread knives, and paring knives.
4. Bakeware such as baking sheets, muffin pans, and cake pans.
5. Small appliances like blenders, food processors, and coffee makers.
6. Dinnerware sets and individual plates, bowls, and mugs.
7. Glassware and barware, including wine glasses, cocktail glasses, and tumblers.
8. Kitchen storage solutions like food containers and pantry organizers.
9. Kitchen linens such as dish towels and aprons.
10. Specialty items like juicers, pasta makers, and slow cookers.

Personalized Gift Category

1. Personalized photo gifts such as mugs, photo albums, and canvas prints
2. Personalized jewelry such as name necklaces and bracelets
3. Personalized home decor such as engraved signs and wall art
4. Personalized clothing such as custom t-shirts and hats
5. Personalized pet products such as custom pet portraits and engraved pet tag

Phone Cases and Accessories

1. Protective phone cases: These are popular as they help to protect phones from scratches, dents, and cracks.
2. Popsockets: These are small circular accessories that attach to the back of a phone case and can be used as a grip, stand or cord wrap.
3. Wireless chargers: With the growing number of wireless charging-capable phones, wireless chargers have become a popular accessory.
4. Screen protectors: Screen protectors help to protect phone screens from scratches, cracks, and shattering.
5. Charging cables: With the constant need to charge phones, charging cables are always in demand.
6. Selfie sticks: These have been popular for a few years now and are still in demand as people love to take group selfies.
7. Phone grips: These are small accessories that attach to the back of a phone case and can be used as a grip to hold the phone more securely.
8. Car phone mounts: These are useful for drivers who use their phones for navigation or hands-free calling.
9. Bluetooth headphones: With more phones removing the headphone jack, Bluetooth headphones have become a popular accessory for those who still want to listen to music or make calls.
10. Phone wallets: These are phone cases that also have a pocket for cards and cash, eliminating the need for a separate wallet.

Sports and Recreation Products

1. Fitness trackers and smartwatches: With a growing interest in fitness and health, fitness trackers and smartwatches that can track heart rate, steps, and calories burned are popular items.
2. Yoga mats: Yoga has gained popularity over the years, and as more people practice it at home, the demand for yoga mats has increased.
3. Resistance bands: Resistance bands are versatile and can be used for a wide range of exercises, making them popular with fitness enthusiasts.
4. Athletic shoes: High-quality athletic shoes that provide support and cushioning during workouts are always in demand.
5. Camping gear: Tents, sleeping bags, and camping accessories are popular items for outdoor enthusiasts.
6. Bicycles and accessories: Bicycles, helmets, and other accessories are popular with both recreational and serious cyclists.
7. Golf equipment: Golf clubs, balls, bags, and other accessories are popular with golf enthusiasts.
8. Sports apparel: Sports jerseys, shorts, and other apparel items are always in demand, particularly for fans of popular sports like football and basketball.
9. Water bottles and hydration packs: As people become more environmentally conscious, reusable water bottles and hydration packs have become popular.
10. Fishing gear: Fishing rods, reels, and accessories are popular with fishing enthusiasts of all levels.

Travel Accessories

1. Packing cubes: These handy cubes help travelers stay organized and maximize space in their luggage.
2. Neck pillows: Neck pillows provide comfort and support during long flights or car rides.
3. Travel adapters: These adapters allow travelers to use their electronic devices in different countries with different power outlets.
4. Luggage scales: A luggage scale helps travelers avoid overweight baggage fees by accurately weighing their luggage before they leave for the airport.
5. Travel-sized toiletries: Small-sized toiletries such as shampoo, conditioner, and toothpaste are convenient for travelers who want to avoid checking a bag or for those who want to save space in their luggage.
6. Portable chargers: These allow travelers to charge their electronic devices on the go, without needing an electrical outlet.
7. Passport holders: A passport holder not only protects your passport but also keeps it organized with additional pockets for credit cards, boarding passes, and other important travel documents.
8. Travel backpacks: A good travel backpack is essential for carrying all of your essentials on the go, whether you're exploring a new city or embarking on a hiking trip.
9. Noise-cancelling headphones: These headphones are perfect for travelers who want to drown out the noise of the plane or surrounding environment and enjoy some peace and quiet.
10. Travel wallets: A travel wallet keeps all your important travel documents, such as your passport and boarding pass, organized in one place for easy access.

Art & Decor Category

1. Canvas Paintings: Canvas paintings are a popular choice for home decor, and there is a huge range of styles and designs available.
2. Wall Stickers and Decals: Wall stickers and decals are an easy and affordable way to add a touch of personality to a room.
3. Sculptures: Sculptures come in many different forms, including abstract and figurative styles. They can be made from a range of materials, from metal and wood to glass and ceramics.
4. Wall Art: Wall art is a great way to add a focal point to a room, and there are many different types available, including framed prints, canvas prints, and posters.
5. Vases and Bowls: Vases and bowls come in a wide range of shapes, sizes, and materials, and can be used to display flowers, fruit, or decorative items.
6. Photo Frames: Photo frames are a great way to display family photos or artwork, and there are many different styles and materials available.
7. Mirrors: Mirrors can be used to create the illusion of more space in a room and can be decorative as well as functional.
8. Clocks: Clocks are both practical and decorative, and there are many different styles and designs available, from classic wall clocks to modern digital ones.
9. Candles and Candle Holders: Candles and candle holders are a great way to add a cozy atmosphere to a room, and there are many different scents and designs available.
10. Rugs and Carpets: Rugs and carpets can add warmth and texture to a room, and there are many different styles and materials available, from wool and cotton to synthetic fibers.

Office Supplies & Stationery

1. Desk organizers and storage units: These are essential for keeping the workspace organized and clutter-free and come in various shapes and sizes to fit different needs.

2. Notebooks and journals: Both for personal and professional use, notebooks and journals remain popular in this category. They can be plain or decorative, and come in a range of sizes and designs.

3. Pens and markers: Pens and markers are a staple in any office or home workspace. From ballpoint pens to gel pens, highlighters, and permanent markers, there are a variety of options available to choose from.

4. Desk accessories: This includes things like tape dispensers, staplers, paper clips, and other office supplies that can add style and functionality to a workspace.

5. Planners and calendars: With busy schedules and deadlines, planners and calendars are a great way to stay organized and keep track of important dates and tasks.

6. Envelopes and mailers: For shipping and sending important documents or packages, envelopes and mailers are essential in any office or home setting.

7. Sticky notes and memo pads: Whether for taking notes, leaving reminders, or brainstorming ideas, sticky notes and memo pads are handy items that can be used in various settings.

8. Stamps and ink pads: For official documents or personal use, stamps and ink pads are important to have on hand. They come in a variety of sizes and designs to fit different needs.

9. File folders and document organizers: To keep important papers and documents organized and easily accessible, file folders and document organizers are a must-have.

10. Printer ink and toner: With the increasing need for remote work and printing from home, printer ink and toner remain a popular item in the office supplies and stationery category.

Musical Instruments & Accessories

1. Guitars: Acoustic and electric guitars, as well as guitar accessories such as strings, picks, and tuners.
2. Keyboards and pianos: Digital keyboards and pianos, as well as accessories such as stands and sustain pedals.
3. Drums and percussion instruments: Drum sets, cymbals, drumsticks, and other percussion instruments.
4. Wind instruments: Saxophones, trumpets, flutes, and clarinets, as well as accessories such as reeds and mouthpieces.
5. String instruments: Violins, cellos, and other stringed instruments, as well as accessories such as bows and rosin.
6. Audio equipment: Microphones, mixers, amplifiers, and other audio equipment used in live performances and recording studios.
7. Music stands and sheet music: Stands for holding sheet music and sheet music books for a variety of instruments and genres.

www.ingramcontent.com/pod-product-compliance
Lightning Source LLC
Chambersburg PA
CBHW071135220526
45467CB00015B/1059